THE PACIFIC BASIN:
AN ECONOMIC HANDBOOK

THE PACIFIC BASIN:
AN ECONOMIC HANDBOOK

EUROMONITOR PUBLICATIONS LIMITED
87–88 Turnmill Street, London EC1M 5QU

THE PACIFIC BASIN:
AN ECONOMIC HANDBOOK
First edition 1987

Other titles in this series:

The African Economic Handbook
The Caribbean Economic Handbook
The Third World Economic Handbook
The East European Economic Handbook
The USSR Economic Handbook
The China Economic Handbook
The South American Economic Handbook
The Middle East Economic Handbook
The Asian Economic Handbook

Published by
Euromonitor Publications Limited
87–88 Turnmill Street
London EC1M 5QU

Telephone: 01–251 8024
Telex: 21120 MONREF G

British Library Cataloguing in Publication Data

Sinclair, Stuart W.
  Pacific Basin Economic Handbook
  1. Pacific Basin —— Economic Conditions
  I. Title
  330.9182'3   HC681

  ISBN 0-86338-139-1

Phototypeset by Photoprint, Torquay, Devon.
Printed in Great Britain by St. Edmundsbury Press, Bury St. Edmunds, Suffolk.

FOREWORD

The latest in Euromonitor's series of economic handbooks explores the dynamic and far-reaching developments currently occurring in the Pacific Basin region and the nations located around the rim of the Pacific Ocean.

The Pacific Basin concept is part of the new world order, a world turned completely around. The East Asian countries, together with Japan, Oceania and the US West Coast are at the forefront of much of the world's technological innovation and industrial development and are the spearhead of current economic growth. Yet this rapid growth has in turn brought social, political and cultural problems and no Pacific Basin economy is without difficulties which pose threats to sustained economic expansion in the future. The strengths and weaknesses of these economies; the complex trade, financial and economic infrastructure of the region, and the challenging new role of the Pacific in the world economy as a whole are the key themes in this major new study.

The handbook is presented in ten chapters, commencing with an overview of the region within a world context and then focusing on a series of major themes including political and economic issues; commodities and commodity trade; energy; financial markets; social issues; manufacturing trends and trade flows. The penultimate chapter considers the future role of the Pacific economy and a detailed statistical datafile concludes the book.

The principal author of *The Pacific Basin: An Economic Handbook* is Stuart Sinclair, who has written extensively on international economic affairs over the last decade and has recently authored *The Third World Economic Handbook*, *The Middle East Economic Handbook* and *The World Petroleum Industry* (all Euromonitor Publications).

Other chapters were contributed by economic writers.

CONTENTS

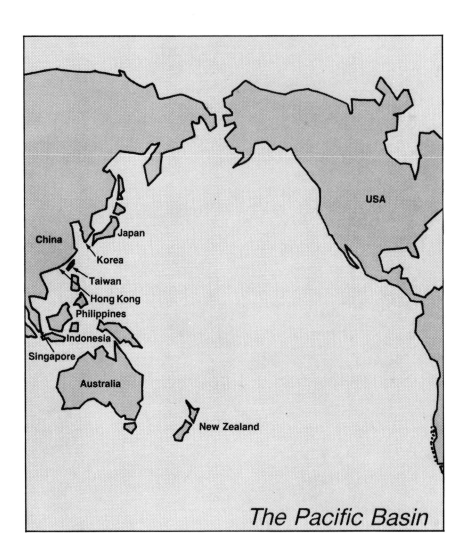

China

Japan

Korea

Taiwan

Hong Kong

Philippines

Indonesia

Singapore

Australia

New Zealand

USA

The Pacific Basin

xii

Chapter One

THE PACIFIC BASIN:
THE REGION AND ITS IMPORTANCE
IN THE WORLD

I What is the Pacific Basin?

The Pacific Basin is composed of 34 countries and accounts for half of the world's population and half of its total wealth. More than a thousand languages are spoken among the 2.4 billion people.

The region is part of the new world order. The East Asian countries, along with California, are in the forefront of much of the world's technological innovation, industrial and product development, and also contribute increasingly to the aesthetics of the rest of the world. The Pacific Basin includes all of the countries which have been in the top ten or so in the world growth rates league since the late 1960s. It includes virtually all those countries which have come to have a significant presence in the world marketplace for a variety of industrial and consumer goods, from shoes and textiles to video-cassette recorders and TV sets and silicon chips. It contains the countries which have tended to display, over the long term, the most judicious approach to economic policy—although none of the fast-growing Pacific Basin countries is without its economic woes. And, perhaps most important, the Pacific Basin contains the first group of developing countries to move towards the level of per capita living standards which, since the second world war, have been enjoyed solely by western Europe, North America, Australia and, latterly, Japan. The small Pacific Basin countries thus represent, in some senses at least, the world's second generation of affluence. That this affluence is not widely shared in all Pacific Basin countries, that it is subject to a number of threats over the next ten or fifteen years, and that its retention is likely to require severe political and economic reform by the year 2000 are some of the themes discussed in this book.

The countries included in this report are the chief economies of the Pacific Basin. The macroeconomic indicators shown in Table 1.1 refer to nine countries, but exclude Mexico and California. Mexico is excluded because its degree of integration with the Pacific economy is as yet relatively modest, measured by trade flows,

1

investment flows and indeed psychological orientation. Moreover, in most respects it is not comparable with the Pacific economies in terms of structure, policy or dynamism. The economy of California is, of course, closely bound up with the Pacific Basin in many ways. Many Asian-based companies have their US headquarters in California. Many Asian-owned financial institutions are in California, while the Californian ports are an important entry for many merchandise exports from Asia. Nonetheless, for obvious reasons, California is not easily treated in the same way as the Pacific economies, and is discussed in this book where relevant, but not as a matter of course. For reference, Table 1.2 shows some macro indicators for these two areas, and for some others in the region which are excluded from this report. The other exclusions, which arguably could be part of the analysis, are Papua New Guinea and Thailand. While Papua New Guinea is clearly relevant on geographical grounds, its economy cannot be said to be integrated into the Pacific. It remains a relatively poor country (1983 GNP per capita was $790), is slow-growing (1.4% annual average GNP growth over the 1973–82 period), and is one in which the patterns of growth and development which typify the dynamic Pacific countries are largely absent. While Thailand is fast-growing and an increasingly sophisticated economy, with private foreign investment increasing, nonetheless it is excluded on the grounds that its location excludes it from the true Pacific Basin economy. As can be seen, there is an arbitrary element in the selection of countries included, but overall the nine countries selected for analysis constitute a reasonable enough balance of geography with economic structure to comprise the core of the Pacific Basin economy.

A sub-set of the Pacific Basin countries is the 'NICs'—the newly industrialising countries. Otherwise known as the Gang of Four, the New Japans and the Four Dragons, this group consists of Hong Kong, South Korea, Singapore and Taiwan. They are distinguished because of their extremely high rates of GNP growth and the ties between them and US and Japanese imports of manufactured goods.

As Table 1.1 suggests, the basic macroeconomic data on the Pacific Basin shows that the region falls into four rough groups—the two countries with settler populations (Australia and New Zealand) which are now grappling with the problems of industrial maturity and agricultural reform; a handful of very fast-growing new

TABLE 1.1   BASIC MACROECONOMIC INDICATORS: KEY ECONOMIES

	GNP at market prices¹		Population ('000)		GNP/capita $US		Growth rates, %			Life expectancy (years)	
	1982	1983	1982	1983	1982	1983	GNP 1973–82	Population 1973–82	GNP/capita 1973–82	1970	1982
Australia	169	166	15,175	15,427	11,140	10,780	2.3	1.3	0.9	71	74
Hong Kong	32	32	5,233	5,313	6,150	6,000	9.5	2.6	6.8	70	75
Indonesia	89	87	152,598	155,824	580	560	7.0	2.3	4.6	47	53
Japan	1,191	1,204	118,449	119,259	10,050	10,100	4.3	1.0	3.3	72	77
South Korea	75	80	39,336	39,958	1,910	2,010	7.2	1.6	5.6	59	67
Malaysia	27	28	14,528	14,863	1,870	1,870	7.4	2.4	4.9	61	67
New Zealand	25	24	3,210	3,237	7,910	7,410	0.4	0.8	-0.3	72	73
Philippines	42	39	50,740	51,980	820	760	5.8	2.8	2.9	59	64
Singapore	15	17	2,472	2,501	5,980	6,620	7.9	1.3	6.5	68	72

Source: *World Bank Atlas*, 1985 Edition
Notes: ¹US$ bn. 1982/83 falls for many countries reflect rise of US dollar more than changes in real economic activity.

TABLE 1.2   BASIC MACROECONOMIC INDICATORS: PERIPHERAL ECONOMIES

	GNP at market prices¹		Population ('000)		GNP/capita $US		Growth rates, %			Life expectancy (years)	
	1982	1983	1982	1983	1982	1983	GNP 1973–82	Population 1973–82	GNP/capita 1973–82	1970	1982
California memo: USA	3,047	3,292	231,533	233,739	13,160	14,090	2.5	1.0	1.5	71	75
Mexico	201	168	73,122	75,103	2,740	2,240	6.2	2.9	3.2	61	65
Papua New Guinea	2.6	2.5	3,128	3,147	830	790	1.4	2.1	-0.7	46	53
Thailand	38	40	48,531	49,568	790	810	6.5	2.4	4.0	58	63

Source: *World Bank Atlas*, 1985 Edition, California data from First Interstate Bank
Note: ¹US$ bn

3

industrial countries, or NICs; other low-income countries which are still heavily involved in raw materials production and trade (Indonesia and Malaysia); and Japan itself. A further group would consist of China alone, for in its population, land mass, development priorities and political infrastructure, China is quite unlike any other country.

The clearest evidence that the Pacific Basin is becoming increasingly important in the world economy comes from the fact that over the past 10 to 15 years these countries have dominated world GNP growth tables. Of the 18 countries which exhibited an annual average growth rate of per capita GNP in excess of 4% over the 1973–82 period, five were in the Pacific Basin (see Table 1.3). Of the seven countries with a growth rate over 6% in the same period, two (Hong Kong and Singapore) were in the Pacific Basin.

TABLE 1.3   RANKINGS OF PER CAPITA GNP GROWTH RATES, 1973–1982

%

	Annual average growth, %
Jordan	11.5
Paraguay	9.4
Hong Kong	6.8
Egypt	6.6
Singapore	6.5
Yemen, PDR	6.4
Saudi Arabia	6.2
Korea	5.6
Hungary	5.6
Oman	5.4
Trinidad & Tobago	5.2
Syria	4.9
Malaysia	4.9
Indonesia	4.6
Cameroon	4.6
China	4.5
Yugoslavia	4.3
Tunisia	4.1

Source: *World Bank Atlas*, 1985 Edition

Chart A shows how Asian countries as a whole enjoyed by far the largest rates of annual GDP growth over the periods 1975–80 and 1981–85. While the Middle East and Latin America saw high growth rates during the early part of the period under study, their growth decelerated severely after 1980, and in the Middle East actually became negative. Only in Asia, moreover, did economic growth accelerate after 1980.

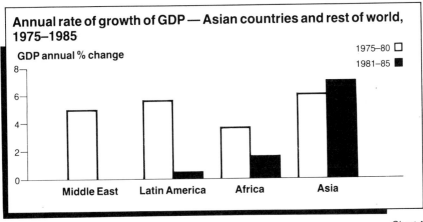

Chart A

Looking at Asia as a rough proxy for the developing world's manufactured goods exporters, Chart B shows that their real GDP

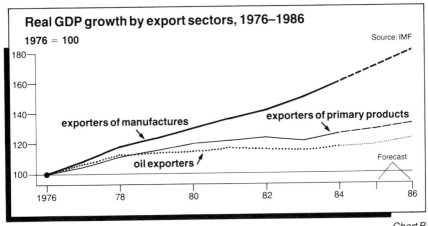

Chart B

5

grew by 80% between 1976 and 1986. Whereas real GDP among oil exporting countries (chiefly this means the 13 members of OPEC) rose by only 21% and in the other raw materials exporting countries by 31%.

A number of factors has contributed to the Asian countries' generally successful economic results. First, economic management by these countries' governments has tended to help overcome, rather than exacerbate, the severe external shocks associated with the oil price rises of 1973–74 and 1979–80. A judicious mixture of fiscal expansion—using government spending to make up for the temporary contraction in private sector spending attributable to the deflationary impact of the oil price increases—with conservative monetary policy, and, later, careful public sector debt management, were characteristics of public policy. While many of these countries' debts remain large they are relatively more manageable than those of the truly large borrowers.

Second, raw materials prices have moved sharply lower, relative to manufactures prices, since 1975, as Chart C shows. By 1985 the terms of trade of the raw materials exporting countries had fallen to about 65% of their 1957 level. Many economists believe that there is a secular raw materials terms of trade decline at work in the world economy, meaning that over time countries which export raw materials will have to give up increasing volumes of them to acquire

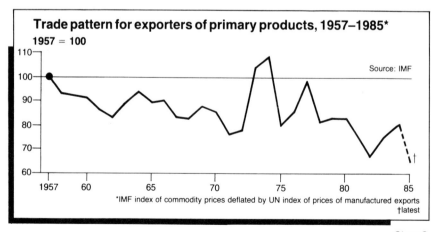

Trade pattern for exporters of primary products, 1957–1985*

1957 = 100

Source: IMF

*IMF index of commodity prices deflated by UN index of prices of manufactured exports
†latest

Chart C

6

a constant amount of manufactured goods imports. To Asian countries with largely manufactured goods exports but high raw material import needs, such as Hong Kong, this development is of course extremely welcome and adds to economic welfare. To Asian countries which rely on raw materials for much of their exports, such as Malaysia and Indonesia, the development is obviously disadvantageous.

One important reason for the considerable interest being aroused by the economies of the Pacific Basin is that to many observers they constitute something of a political and economic experiment. In the NICs in particular, it is argued that governments have tended to allow market forces to determine many aspects of the economy. For instance, urban planning has tended—until recently, at least—to be sketchy, and has erected few zoning restrictions to obstruct the wishes of manufacturers and builders. Laws regarding wages and trade unions have tended to reinforce the free market.

This view has, however, tended to be accepted too uncritically by outside observers. For the fact is that many Asian governments do intervene widely in their economies. In Hong Kong, for instance, the New Territories are dotted with public housing built for low-income residents, often new emigrants from mainland China, who found that housing was virtually unaffordable after Hong Kong's real estate booms of the 1970s and early 1980s. In Japan, government intervention is legendary, of course, and involves elaborate restrictions on such areas as requirements placed on importers, the managed and co-ordinated reductions in capacity in certain industries—notably shipbuilding and aluminium smelting, and in the overseas bond purchases made by the major banks. In Singapore, official policy decisions made in the late 1970s were responsible for forcing wages up faster than they would otherwise have moved, in order to shift the economy away from labour-intensive activities as fast as possible. In South Korea, governments have targeted certain sectors of the economy, such as shipbuilding and automobiles, as growth sectors and have actively managed corporate mergers and restructurings within each sector. South Korean governments have brought to bear a wide array of subsidies and other capital inducements to help entrepreneurs in such sectors grow rapidly. The South Korean government also offers five-year tax holidays and 100% depreciation allowances for foreign companies investing in selected industries, which recently have included computer disks, electronic appliances for the media industry, electric motors and so on. Fewer sectors are now banned to foreign investors, with 133 sectors being taken off the 'negative list' during 1985, so that about 80% of South Korean industrial categories can now have foreign participation. In Malaysia too there has been extensive public intervention, much of it concerned with redistributing economic opportunity between the country's racial groups. Throughout Asia, then, the picture which emerges is not so much that of dynamic and totally unregulated economies as that of economies with tendencies to dynamic growth, but with that growth shaped and sometimes tightly circumscribed by government decisions. The Pacific Basin as the vindication of pure laissez-faire economic policy is thus a myth; rather, the region has tended to show the forcefulness of a judicious mixture of private enterprise and public policy.

II The Pacific Basin and the world economy

The Pacific Basin possesses 21% of the world's oil resources, 63% of its wool, 67% of its cotton, 87% of its natural rubber and 94% of its natural silk.

Perhaps the characteristic which has most clearly distinguished the small Pacific Basin countries in the last 10 to 15 years has been their explosive export performance. As chart D shows, Hong Kong, Singapore, Taiwan and South Korea (with Japan not far behind) have consistently led the field in annual export growth, as measured by GATT. Comparing this export performance with growth of real GDP shows a fairly strong positive relationship between the two. During the period 1973–84, as analysed by GATT, six countries entered the table of the world's twenty largest exporting countries— South Korea, China, Hong Kong, Taiwan, Mexico and Singapore. These countries displaced Australia, Poland, Denmark, Iran, Czechoslovakia and the GDR. As one commentator on the GATT statistics put it, 'the distinction between developing and developed countries among leading exporters of manufactures is becoming blurred. By 1984 Taiwan and South Korea, for instance, had overtaken Switzerland and Sweden.'

Tables 1.4 to 1.8 show various aspects of Pacific Basin trade.

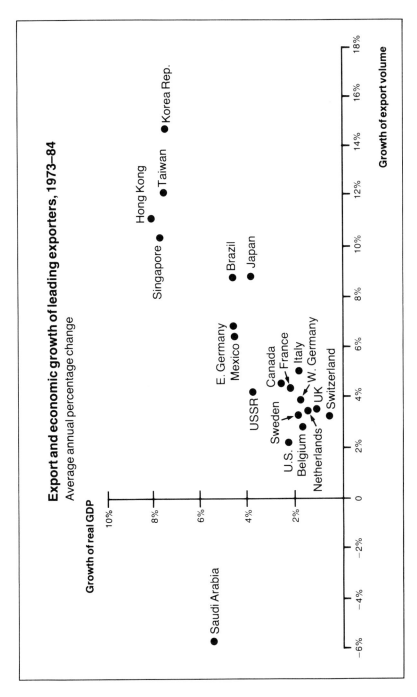

Export and economic growth of leading exporters, 1973–84
Average annual percentage change

Growth of real GDP

Growth of export volume

Chart D

9

From Table 1.4 it is apparent that textiles and clothing alone account for high shares of several countries' exports by value; Hong Kong and South Korea have particularly high concentrations of exports in these categories. Machinery and transport equipment are increasingly important for many countries: Hong Kong, Japan, South Korea, Malaysia and Singapore have all recorded significant increases in the share of their exports accounted for by these categories over the past 17 years. Primary commodities, other than fuels, mineral and metals, have been declining in importance for all countries, in some cases quite sharply. As far as the composition of their imports is concerned, the Asian countries exhibited a sharp increase in the importance of fuels over the 1965–82 period, due to increasing volumes and unit values of oil imports. Since 1980–81, on the other hand, these figures will have fallen. The importance of food in total imports is falling in all countries bar Indonesia. (This has occurred despite vigorous growth in per capita food output in Indonesia.) Machinery and transport equipment accounted for over 25% of imports by value in five countries in 1982; and for over 20% of imports in eight countries. This implies that capital goods imports are increasingly important in most of these countries—exactly as would be expected in a high-growth environment. (Two exceptions to this rule are the Philippines, where the weighting of this category has declined markedly, and Japan, where a slight decline is almost certainly attributable to more use of domestic suppliers of these goods.)

Both imports and exports have been growing strongly in the majority of these countries. As Table 1.5 shows, only in two cases (Australia and Indonesia) did exports in the 1973–83 period rise less quickly than in the industrial market economies. In many cases exports grew twice as fast or more. Import growth was similarly robust. The value of imports grew faster than the value of exports in three countries, while the reverse was true in four countries.

As far as inter-regional trade patterns are concerned, Tables 1.6 and 1.7 show how the industrial market economies were by far the most important trade partners of all the Asian countries except Singapore in 1965, and how this dominance had fallen for most of them by 1983. East Europe has never been more than a marginal trade partner. The OPEC countries were very significant markets for a number of Pacific countries, in construction projects and pure

TABLE 1.4 STRUCTURE OF INTERNATIONAL TRADE

% share of merchandise exports

	Fuels, minerals, metals		Other prim. commodities		Textiles & clothing		Machinery % transport/equipment		Other manufactures	
	1965	1982	1965	1982	1965	1982	1965	1982	1965	1982
Australia	13	37	73	41	1	1	5	5	9	16
Hong Kong	2	2	11	6	43	34	6	19	37	39
Indonesia	43	85	53	11	—	1	3	1	1	2
Japan	2	1	7	2	17	4	31	56	43	36
South Korea	15	1	25	7	27	21	3	28	29	43
Malaysia	35	35	59	42	—	3	2	15	4	5
New Zealand	1	5	94	71	1	2	—	8	4	15
Philippines	11	12	84	38	1	7	—	3	5	39
Singapore	21	30	44	13	6	4	10	26	18	28

% share of merchandise imports

	Food		Fuels		Other prim. commodities		Machinery % transport/equipment		Other manufactures	
	1965	1982	1965	1982	1965	1982	1965	1982	1965	1982
Australia	6	5	8	14	9	3	37	39	41	38
Hong Kong	26	14	3	8	11	5	13	22	46	52
Indonesia	6	7	3	21	2	5	39	38	50	29
Japan	23	13	20	50	38	16	9	6	11	15
South Korea	15	12	7	30	26	15	13	23	38	20
Malaysia	27	12	12	15	7	5	22	40	32	29
New Zealand	8	7	7	17	9	5	33	33	43	39
Philippines	20	10	10	26	7	4	33	22	30	38
Singapore	24	8	13	34	18	4	14	28	30	26

Source: *World Bank Atlas*, 1985 Edition

TABLE 1.5   AVERAGE ANNUAL GROWTH OF MERCHANDISE TRADE

%

	Exports		Imports		Terms of trade (1980=100)	
	1965–73	1973–83	1965–73	1973–83	1965–73	1973–83
Australia	9.3	2.7	6.8	—	100	97
Hong Kong	11.7	10.3	10.5	12.0	97	—
Indonesia	11.1	1.4	13.9	9.8	110	102
Japan	14.7	7.4	14.9	1.3	103	106
South Korea	31.7	14.8	22.4	7.5	93	100
Malaysia	8.0	4.9	4.4	7.3	91	87
New Zealand	6.0	4.4	4.0	0.1	99	96
Philippines	4.2	7.5	3.1	1.3	88	92
Singapore	11.0	—	9.8	—	—	—
Taiwan	—	—	—	—	—	—

Source: *World Bank Atlas*, 1985 Edition
Memo: industrial market economies
Memo: upper middle income countries

TABLE 1.6   ORIGIN AND DESTINATION OF MERCHANDISE IMPORTS

% of total

	Industrial market economies		East European economies		High-income oil exporters		Developing countries	
	1965	1983	1965	1983	1965	1983	1965	1983
Australia	69	60	4	3	1	3	26	34
Hong Kong	67	61	—	—	1	3	32	35
Indonesia	72	73	5	1	—	1	23	26
Japan	49	50	3	2	2	8	47	39
South Korea	75	65	0	—	—	10	25	25
Malaysia	56	50	7	3	—	1	36	47
New Zealand	88	64	1	5	—	2	11	30
Philippines	95	77	0	2	—	1	5	20
Singapore	28	42	6	1	2	5	64	52

Source: World Bank Atlas, 1985 edition

12

TABLE 1.7 ORIGIN AND DESTINATION OF MERCHANDISE EXPORTS

	Industrial market economies		East European economies		High-income oil exporters		Developing countries		Manufactured exports ($ mn)	
	1965	1982	1965	1982	1965	1982	1965	1982	1965	1982
Australia	57	35	—	—	—	2	43	63	432	4,736
Hong Kong	71	62	—	—	1	4	28	34	995	19,277
Indonesia	25	42	1	—	—	7	74	51	27	868
Japan	47	48	2	3	2	8	49	41	7,704	134,209
South Korea	68	62	0	0	—	11	32	27	104	19,237
Malaysia	17	67	—	—	2	2	81	31	75	2,781
New Zealand	90	70	—	1	—	1	10	28	53	1,322
Philippines	93	75	0	—	—	1	7	23	43	2,492
Singapore	9	49	—	1	3	6	88	44	338	11,834

Source: *World Bank Atlas*, 1985 Edition

manpower exports as well as in merchandise trade, although since 1982 or 1983 this market has shrunk appreciably. South Korea has experienced the largest growth in this regard over the 18-year period. After 1983, however, with the scaling back of most OPEC countries' development plans, trade diminished. Other developing countries were increasingly important as trade partners for many Asian countries. By 1983 the lowest proportion of any country's exports going to other developing countries was that of the Philippines, at 20%.

In trade in manufactured goods alone, as shown in Table 1.7, the industrial market economies have been of diminishing importance for all Asian countries except Indonesia, Japan, Malaysia and Singapore. Developing countries, by contrast, have grown in importance, and by 1982 were absorbing over 30% of the manufactured goods exports of Australia, Hong Kong, Indonesia, Japan, Malaysia and Singapore. In 1965 this proportion was reached by Australia, Indonesia, Japan, South Korea, Malaysia and Singapore, suggesting that in Hong Kong and South Korea manufactures exports were increasingly sent to oil exporting countries and to industrial market economies.

Trade within the Asian countries is shown in Table 1.8. The table shows that the importance of intra-Asian trade has grown for three of the countries, but not for Taiwan, over the 1975–84 period. It

TABLE 1.8 ASIAN REGIONAL TRADE FLOWS, 1975–1984

% distribution of exports

Source	1975	1981	1984
Hong Kong[1]			
including China	13	21	24
excluding China	12	12	13[2]
South Korea	8	11	12[2]
Singapore	40	42	42[2]
Taiwan	17	17	14

Source: *Far East Economic Review*
Notes: [1]includes re-exports   [2]1983 not 1984

should be remembered, however, that the growth underlying this distribution is very rapid in absolute terms, so that the dollar value of trade between Taiwan and the other countries continues to rise.

III   The Pacific Basin and the USA

The Pacific Basin countries have been drawn closer and closer to the US economy during the 1970s and 1980s through trade. As Table 1.9 shows, the trend over the 1982–85 period has been for the US to take a rising proportion of exports from all the countries listed. For the past eight years US trade in the Pacific has outstripped trade across the Atlantic to Europe. In the cases of Hong Kong, Japan, South Korea, Philippines and Taiwan, the US market absorbs over one-third of their total exports (by value).

TABLE 1.9   PACIFIC BASIN COUNTRIES' EXPORTS TO THE US AS % OF TOTAL EXPORTS 1982–1985, AND % GROWTH OF EXPORTS, 1980–1984

Country	% growth of exports, 1980–84	As % of total export growth, 1980–84	1982	1983	1984	1985[1]
Australia	—	—	10	10	11	12
China	191	30	8.1	5.7	9.3	9.4
Hong Kong	77	41	29	32	44	39
Indonesia	7	(a)	16	20	21	21
Japan	83	65	26	29.2	35.3	37
South Korea	126	54	29	34	36	37
Malaysia	5	19	12	13	14	14
Philippines	—	—	32	36	38	39
Singapore	108	56	13	18	20	21
Taiwan	119	78	39.5	45.1	48.8	5

Sources: US Dept of Commerce, IMF
Notes: [1]Forecasts for 1985 by Business International
        (a)Total exports fell over the 1980–84 period

What drives the growth of these exports? Three different factors are responsible. One is price: the fact that these Asian countries have collectively been becoming increasingly competitive sources to buy goods which were previously made in the US or imported from elsewhere—say, Europe. There is a fairly straightforward substitution of sourcing due to price. A second phenomenon would be product composition—the notion that Asian suppliers happened to be able to provide the type of goods for which demand in the US was increasing. There seems to be evidence for this line of argument in the case of certain electronics goods such as VCRs, early designs for which were virtually only found in Japan and, later, South Korea and Taiwan. A third factor at work could be more institutional in nature—multinational companies arranged an increasing volume of their sourcing in Asian countries, so that some of the trade being recorded in the data is 'captive' imports, or imports already sold. Countries without multinational operations could also be involved in this, with sub-contracting or other sourcing arrangements in Asian countries having been made in advance of the actual flow of goods taking place.

Almost all Pacific countries record trae surpluses with the US (which tend to compensate for their deficits with Japan). Japan has by far the largest surplus with the US, at around US$ 50 bn, which has grown from US$ 20 bn in 1983. Other Pacific economies with growing surpluses are Taiwan, South Korea and Hong Kong, however the resource-rich ASEAN states have experienced a slower growth as primary commodity exports such as palm oil, rubber and natural gas weakened.

The Pacific census region (which includes California, Washington State, Oregon, Alaska and Hawaii) had 34.2 mn inhabitants in 1984, up from 26.5 mn in 1970. This made it the fourth-largest census region in the US, and in terms of percentage population growth over the 1970–80 period the Pacific ranked fourth again. Over the 1980–84 period the Pacific region's population grew at an annual average rate of 1.8%, as against 1.0% for the US as a whole, but well below the 2.5% rate achieved by the Mountain region of the US. Measured by rate of nonfarm employment growth, the Pacific was the third-fastest growing region over the 1970–84 period. Employment grew by 3.67% per year over 1970–80 and by 1.41% per year over 1980–84, as against increases for the whole of the US of 2.46% and 1.02% respectively.

16

In California, taken on its own, nonfarm employment grew by 5.9% between 1983 and 1984, while between 1984 and 1986 nonfarm employment there is forecast by the State of California to grow from 10.57 mn to 11.38 mn. Californian personal income should grow faster than the US average, to reach $429.8 bn by 1986, equivalent to 12.3% of total US income. This will maintain California's position as having the largest gross state income of any state in the US.

Data on trade between California and the Pacific are not readily obtainable. Estimates of total trade by customs district are, however, available, and point to the west taking an increasing share

TABLE 1.10 US WEST COAST INVOLVEMENT IN INTERNATIONAL TRADE, 1984–1985

	First half, 1984	$ mn 1985	Change, $ mn	1984–85 %
Exports				
Portland	1,997	1,888	−109	−5.5
San Francisco	6,051	5,927	−124	−2.1
Los Angeles	9,276	10,767	1,492	16.1
San Diego	686	786	100	14.6
Honolulu	172	164	−8.6	−5.0
West Coast	24,773	27,381	2,659	10.8
Total USA	108,690	110,468	1,778	1.6
West Coast as % of US	22.8	24.8		
Imports				
Portland	1,768	1,899	132	7.5
San Francisco	7,818	7,743	−75	−1.0
Los Angeles	16,374	23,041	6,666	41
San Diego	748	868	120	16.0
Honolulu	837	811	−26	−3.0
West Coast	36,555	44,092	7,537	20.6
Total USA	123,522	127,419	3,897	3.2
West Coast as % of US	29.7	34.5		

Source: First Interstate Bank, Los Angeles

17

of all US imports and exports. Table 1.10 shows, for instance, that California is an increasingly important point of entry for goods entering the US.

California's international trade has trebled since 1970 and accounts for around a fifth of the state's GNP compared to a tenth a decade ago. About 75% of its international trade is with Pacific Basin countries.

Another piece of evidence which confirms the growing ties between the US and the Pacific are recent data on US bank lending. Excluding Japan, the Pacific Basin accounted for 40% of total international capital commitments of US banks in 1984. The total capital inflow to these countries was $38.5 bn. Including Japan, the total was 88% or $85 bn.

Total US investment in the Asia/Pacific region increased by $3,353 mn in 1984, as shown in Table 1.11. Cumulative US direct foreign investment at end-1984 stood at $233.4 bn, with the Asia/Pacific share of that 15%. The largest share remains that of Europe, with 45.5% of the total; Canada, with 22.1%, has the second-largest share and Asia/Pacific the third. Indonesia received the largest US investment inflow in 1984, with $1.2 bn being placed. Hong Kong was the second most important recipient; $489 mn was invested

TABLE 1.11   CHANGES IN US DIRECT INVESTMENT, 1984

Region	Change in investment stock, $mn
Asia/Pacific	3,353
Canada	2,914
Africa (not South Africa)	1,028
Europe	974
Middle East	388
South Africa	−493
Latin America	−1,580

Source: US Dept of Commerce

there. Much of the investment in Indonesia is going to petroleum-related projects, while in Hong Kong nearly half the funds are allocated to trade-related projects. The other recipients, in descending order, were Australia (which experienced a $432 mn inflow), Japan ($311 mn), Singapore ($263 mn), Thailand ($237 mn), South Korea ($173 mn), Taiwan ($127 mn), the Philippines ($78 mn) and Malaysia ($32 mn). In New Zealand investment fell by $55 mn, equivalent to about a 10% divestment.

Looking at US banks' assets in Pacific Basin countries, as indicated in Table 1.12, shows that South Korea accounts for by far the biggest outstanding loans in the non-rescheduling developing countries category. (Compare South Korea's loans of $11.1 bn from all US banks to their lending exposure in Mexico, for instance, at $25.8 bn or Brazil at $24.8 bn in 1985). The governments and other public sector agencies of these countries have been active borrowers in recent years. The South Korean public sector borrowed an additional $887 mn from US banks in 1984, for instance, raising its borrowing by 60%. In Malaysia public sector debt grew by $581 mn. In South Korea private borrowings grew by $637 mn in the same period. The significant increases and decreases in US banks' asset positions with Pacific Basin economies are shown in Table 1.13.

TABLE 1.12   US BANK LENDING IN PACIFIC BASIN COUNTRIES: MARCH 1985 EXPOSURES

	Lending $ mn	As % of capital
South Korea	11,140.6	11.53
Taiwan	3,142.6	3.25
Indonesia	3,092.3	3.20
Malaysia	1,935.9	2.00
China	1,237.1	1.28

Source: American Express

Notes   Figures refer to March 1985 asset lending by all US banks. Total US bank lending overseas at date was $330.8 bn.

TABLE 1.13   US BANKS' MAIN PORTFOLIO CHANGES IN PACIFIC BASIN ECONOMIES, 1982–1985

Country	Asset position June 1982	US$ mn March 1985	1982–85 %	Change rank
Japan	42,056	46,736	+11.13	First
South Korea	9,214	11,141	+20.92	Fifth
Indonesia	2,360	3,092	+31.00	Seventh
Malaysia	1,346	1,936	+43.83	Eighth
Hong Kong	5,189	3,865	−25.52	Sixth (fall)
Taiwan	4,447	3,143	−29.33	Seventh (fall)

Source: American Express

IV   China enters the Pacific Basin economy

China's integration to the Pacific economy is proceeding, chiefly through trade, with direct foreign investment remaining at very low levels. This is particularly evident with regard to China's major trading partner, Japan, which is quite willing to enhance trading volumes but reluctant to invest. China's political stability is as yet unproven.

China has become an important trading partner for Hong Kong and Japan and recently with Taiwan. In the case of Hong Kong, trade patterns have become much more complex and sophisticated in recent years. China used to sell raw materials, fuel and foodstuffs to Hong Kong, with that flow yielding about 30% of China's hard currency earnings. Now, a huge variety of goods passes between the two.

Since 1978, Hong Kong's exports and re-exports to China have grown by 10,000%, from HK$ 81 mn in 1978 to HK$ 11.3 bn in 1984 for exports, and from HK$ 214 mn to HK$ 28 bn for re-exports. Imports from China have risen from HK$ 10.5 bn in 1978 to HK$ 56 bn in 1984. Chinese authorities have made some highly-publicised investments, such as the new Bank of China headquarters building. Hong Kong companies, for their part, have accounted for 90% of all investment by foreigners in China's 'special economic zones'.

In the case of Japan, exports to China have grown so quickly that the deficit of $2 bn recorded in 1982 has been transformed to a surplus of nearly $4 bn. Goods in particularly strong demand in China have been TV sets and automobiles. In the latter market sector, China is now the second biggest export market for Japanese producers after the US.

Many international oil companies are bidding for new oil exploration licences, with early seismic tests yielding extremely good results.

Trade between China and Taiwan also appears to be growing apace. Although this trade is not recorded officially—while not strictly illegal, it is not officially sanctioned either—all the evidence suggests that it is rising extremely rapidly. In 1984, Taiwanese companies exported an estimated $430 mn. Chinese companies are thought to have exported about $270 mn-worth of goods to Taiwan. These volumes represent more than a doubling since 1983. For 1985, estimates of the value of the countries' two-way trade exceed $1 bn. In the first quarter, Taiwan's exports to China may have been in the order of $800 mn. Although this is a modest share of Taiwan's total exports (which in 1984 were worth some $30.5 bn), such export diversification is always welcome, and in this case particularly desirable insofar as it helps defuse tensions between the two states.

Official trade ties between Indonesia and China were established in 1985. Flows between the two countries are estimated to be worth about $300 mn per year.

As China effectively only opened its doors to international trade under 10 years ago it will take some time for its economy to be mobilised into becoming self-sufficient and a net exporter in manufacturing terms, although successes have been achieved in the agricultural sector as China is now a net exporter of grains and exporter of cotton.

However, China's size means that any gradual shifts will have a significant impact on trade flows around the Pacific and further afield.

Chapter Two

POLITICAL AND ECONOMIC ISSUES
IN THE PACIFIC BASIN

I Introduction

The purpose of this chapter is to offer a brief review of the major
economic and political factors at work in each of the Pacific Basin
countries. The countries are grouped into four categories, reflecting
more economic similarities than any common political aspects:-
— Japan
— NICs Hong Kong, South Korea, Singapore and Taiwan, i.e.
   the small manufacture-exporting developing countries.
— Indonesia, Malaysia and Philippines, i.e. primary commodity
   production and trade countries.
— Australia and New Zealand.

Politically, Japan, Australia, New Zealand, Malaysia and Singapore would be grouped together as democracies or emerging
democracies whereas Taiwan, Philippines, Korea and Indonesia
could be termed as military regimes or recently liberated from
military rule.

Despite the heterogeneity of these Pacific Basin economies, there
is a number of common factors shared between them. Many of these
are external: they involve trade relations with the main non-Pacific
trade partner, the United States, as well as intra-Pacific relations
such as those between the NICs and Japan. There is also the shared
concern of a multilateral defence, and the question of how closely
and in what ways the Pacific nations should try to shelter beneath
the umbrella of the United States defence apparatus. There are also
shared concerns of a sociological nature, such as the way political
institutions are going to evolve in many of the countries. While
economic growth in many has been impressive, there has been no
commensurate increase in political institution-building. In some
cases, such as central banking and the development of sophisticated
capital markets and other monetary institutions, this failure may
have serious consequences in the next few years.

II   Japan

Political scene

Politics in Japan are highly factionalised. (See Table 2.1.) There are five main factions: Tanaka; Suzuki; Fukuda; Nakasone; Komoto. Elections for prime minister are held every three years and the next one is due at the end of 1987.

Yasuhiro Nakasone, the current Prime Minister, has broken the mould of Japanese politicians. He is a leader rather than a follower, a flouter of taboos who perceives his mission as the tearing-down of the post-World War II Japanese pacifist position and the establishment of distinct and aggressive Japanese foreign policy.

Mr. Nakasone is a right-winger who would like to rewrite Japan's 1946 'peace constitution' to build a stronger army, double defence spending, revive the status of the Emperor, and promote a new nationalism in Japanese schools. His ideal foreign policy would resemble France's: pro-western but fiercely independent.

Like his western counterpart, Ronald Reagan, Mr. Nakasone is an adept manipulator of the media who is popular more for his personal style, which has become closely identified with a recovery of Japanese national pride and sense of direction, than for his ideas.

TABLE 2.1   JAPAN: POLITICAL FACTIONS BY NUMBERS

LDP factions	House of representatives	House of councillors	Total	PM candidate
Tanaka	65	53	118	Takeshita
Suzuki	52	29	81	Miyazawa
Fukuda	47	25	72	Abe
Nakasone	49	16†	65	Nakasone
Komoto	26	6	32	
Independent	18	12	30	

Source: Business press

Note: †Called Mokuyo, or Thursday Club, because Tanaka quit LDP after bribery scandal in 1976. Includes five opportunists who belong to other factions.

Even his own Liberal Democratic Party flatly refused formally to rescind the 1% of GNP ceiling set on defence spending, a policy set by the Takeo Miki cabinet in 1976 and now a sacrosanct symbol of pacifist resistance to military resurgence. This was considered a humiliating political defeat but Nakasone managed to rise above it.

Some western protectionist politicians have labelled Nakasone an opportunist, but his achievements have been considerable. He has patched up Japan's tetchy trade relations with South Korea, initiated an aggressive foreign aid programme to shore up Japan's alliances throughout the Pacific Basin and Southeast Asia, established better control over the bureaucracy and placed more top officials abroad. In general he has pushed the insular and chauvinistic Japanese into establishing more in the way of a distinct foreign policy than they have ever had before. Most important, he has kept the lid on Japan's volatile trade relations with the United States at a time when protectionist pressures in the US have threatened to blow it off. At the same time, he has also managed to defuse long-held tensions with the Soviet Union over the disputed territorial claims on the islands of Shikotan, Etorofu, Kunashiro and the Habomais which lie just north of Hokkaido and the disputed Soya Straits; and to renegotiate trade relations with that nation.

Economic scene

Japan has given the world its greatest post-war success story. Devastated by World War II, the Japanese had a choice of working or starving. Sustained by an intensely cohesive culture in which co-operation is highly valued, the Japanese worked very hard. Today, they supply two-thirds of the world market for large computer memory chips, and 90% of the market for large mass-production chips. Japanese companies produce the VHS and Beta video formats which have made video-cassette recorders the largest-selling of all consumer electrical goods. Japanese shipyards build more than half the world's ships. The Japanese car industry has devastated all of its competitors, and Japanese management practices have become the envy and the admiration of the western world.

Japan is the only fully industrialised of all the Asian economies. As such, it is an important part of the world trade environment, but even more so for its Pacific neighbours. It is a major export market,

25

absorbing up to one-half of their exports and providing most of their imports of manufactured goods. At the same time, trade with the Asian countries accounts for more than one-quarter of Japan's exports and imports. Trade between Japan and its Asian neighbours has been more than twice as intense as their world trade shares would lead one to expect. However, these close trade relationships do not appear to be founded so much on comparative advantage as on geographic proximity, market familiarity, and in certain cases such as Malaysia, direct foreign investment.

Trade relationship with the US

However, it is with the United States that Japan has formed its closest trade link. Together, they have created a joint economy known as the 'Nichibei economy' (a blend of the Japanese characters for Japan, or Nihon, and America, Beikoku or rice country), which accounts for about one-third of the world's entire GNP. Since 1982, Japan has supplied goods for America's boom while America has supplied markets for Japan's growth. Currently, one-third of Japan's exports go to America, while more than 20% of America's exports go to Japan. America's chief export to Japan is food such as grains, beef and citrus. Japan's chief exports are automobiles and electronic consumer goods.

Since 1983, America and Japan have been the two fastest-growing countries in the industrialised world, with 4% of real GNP growth each in that year, then 6.8% for America and 5.8% for Japan in 1984. However, despite the trade interdependence the US has been running a series of substantial trade deficits whilst Japan correspondingly records ever-increasing trade surpluses.

This is in part due to the weakness of the yen against the dollar in recent years, exacerbated by US fiscal policy which has kept the budget deficit high, pushing interest rates up and sucking in capital from abroad to compensate for the low national savings rate. An agreement among five advanced nations known as the Group of Five in September of 1985 brought down the value of the dollar against the yen, causing Japanese companies to readjust their export-oriented policies of the past. However, it is expected that the process of realignment will take a long time and will rely on many factors more complex than the juggling of exchange rates.

26

Part of the problem is that Japan's economic policy is diametrically opposed to that of the United States, providing the spectacle of two nations divided by a common economy. Japanese government is committed to the twin dragons of fiscal austerity and administrative reform (meaning small government and the privatisation of public enterprise). Between 1980 and 1985, it slashed the overall deficit from over 7% to below 3%. In seven years, Japanese consumer prices have risen by 30% while America's have risen by 60%. Average productivity rose by 27%, slightly more than in America. The American current-account deficit is continuing to rise beyond $120 bn, while Japan's surplus exceeds $45 bn.

These inequities have produced serious strains between the two nations. 1985 saw more protectionist bills pending in Congress than in the past fifty years put together. Most of these were aimed at forcing Japan to consume more American goods, or to inhibit sales of Japanese goods in the United States. To date, President Reagan has vetoed all of them, but one bill passed by President Carter in 1981 is still in force and sets a ceiling of two million cars per year on Japanese auto imports.

Over the long run one answer to the problem is more trade instead of less, and to a certain extent it is already being addressed by the increasing proportion of Japanese investment in American manufacturing. According to the Japanese Economic Institute, Japanese firms had stakes of 50% or more in 342 American manufacturers by the end of 1984. The largest is Nippon Kohan's 50% share in National Steel, America's sixth-largest steel maker. Investment is heaviest in the areas of car manufacture and electronics, and most widespread in California, Washington state, Illinois, and underpopulated southern states such as Tennessee and Kentucky, where Toyota and Nissan are providing tremendous boosts with their large new plants. However, this trend is arguably having a negative impact on the Asian economies, which are losing the manufacturing business, and also on the consumer who may end up paying higher prices for his goods.

Domestic economy

Japan's growth rate in 1985 was 4.5%, a respectable figure though down from 5.8% in 1984. In the area of investment, expansion slowed but remained strong in high technology. Wages rose by 5% while prices rose by only 3.5%, giving a boost to consumer expenditure. There was a current-account surplus of more than $45 bn, with similar figures projected for 1986 by government analysts. However, outsiders are raising fundamental questions about the long-term strength of the economy, with a sharp falling-off perhaps as early as 1986 due to the impact of trade restrictions on Japan.

In the last decade private and public sector co-operation has helped Japan cut more basic and less profitable industries such as aluminium and coal production, textiles, shipbuilding and steel. The video-cassette boom is peaking although laser-read discs are poised to take their place. The petro-chemical industry, which suffered heavy losses in the early 1980s, is undergoing a 10-to-15-year restructuring. And indeed, Japan's entire communications system will be replaced over the next eleven years by the Information Network System, a vast undertaking, perhaps the last great national project of the century, which will link telephones, television, facsimile machines, computers, offices, homes, banks and supermarkets.

As China and South Korea concentrate on cars, ships and televisions, Japan is devoting its efforts to miracle drugs, software and infinite magnitudes of memory chips. Among the areas of research commanding most attention in semiconductor research are complimentary metal oxide semiconductors (CMOS), which offer improved data-storage capacity through low-power consumption; and gallium arsenide (GaAS), which offers dramatic improvements in processing speeds. Japan is considered to be conducting 70% of GaAs research worldwide.

Other innovations include Toshiba's 1 megabit (million bit) DRAM memory chip, and a 100-megabit chip which will take five years to develop.

Another innovative trend may point to some basic changes in the heart of Japanese business life itself. In Japan, qualified people have tended to work for large, established corporations with job security and up-to-date facilities. But now a growing number of engineers and computer programmers is leaving to join smaller firms known as 'second-venture businesses', claiming big corporations offer less challenge and less job satisfaction. Second-venture businesses are small start-up companies in the fields of high technology, publishing, services and consumer finance. Estimates of their numbers range from 5,000 (government figures) to less than 500.

Overall, the very conservatism which played such a large part in creating Japan's success story may become an impediment to the country's further development. In 1976, the government decided to impose a ceiling of 1% of the GNP on defence spending; this is now inadequate to maintain even Japan's limited defence goals. (By contrast, West Germany spends 4% of GNP per year on defence, and Australia 3%). Japan's current economic growth rate means that defence spending can potentially increase by 4–5% per year, but it is unlikely that this cushion will be utilised in full due to Japan's continuing sensitivity to being perceived as a militaristic nation.

An overly-cautious approach may already be slowing Japan's hitherto spectacular growth. Government optimism regarding current figures appears to be more of an effort to save face in the absence of effective measures to increase domestic demand. As net exports fall in the face of US protectionism, growth in Japan in 1986 may be the lowest since immediately after the first oil shock in 1973. This slow growth could make it impossible for the government to achieve its long-standing goal of reducing the dependence of the central government on deficit-covering bond issues. Since 1983, when the government first identified fiscal stability as its top priority in macro-economic policy, the Ministry of Finance has been trying to reduce the budget deficit by an average of Y1 trillion per year. But the slow growth, ironically combined with wished-for low inflation, means that tax revenue will grow too slowly for this programme to be adhered to.

III The NICs—an overview

The four small, fast-growing, manufacture-exporting economies of the Pacific Basin are Hong Kong, South Korea, Singapore and Taiwan. They share a number of characteristics, as outlined in Chapter 1: these include very rapid post-war growth of GNP, rapid evolution of their industrial sectors from simple, labour-intensive processing to a wide range of high value-added goods. Although the dominant industries in the NICs continue to be clothing, apparel and footwear, in these sectors the types of goods being exported are orientated more towards the sophisticated end of the market, with production of the more basic items being ceded to lower wage locations such as the Philippines, Pakistan and Sri Lanka. In Singapore, refined oil and shipbuilding dominated until the late 1970s; however, these sectors were replaced with a variety of electronic-based activities including hardware assembly and software development.

In all four NICs there is a feeling that 1984–1986 marks a turning-point. What is needed to resume the rapid growth of earlier decades is a judicious mixture of public and private policy measures designed to facilitate adjustment to a world of more intense competition in manufactured goods, and of tougher access to most of the world's major markets.

IV Hong Kong

Political scene

Hong Kong has experienced prolonged and at times acute political uncertainty over Sino-British sovereignty negotiations which began in 1984. In 1985, China and Britain signed a joint declaration in which Britain promised to return the territory to Peking in 1997, thereby ending twenty years of dispute. The British, having won Hong Kong in 1841, retained control of the vital entrepôt after World War II and the communist takeover of mainland China, and refused to give it back despite repeated demands for its return by the Chinese.

The majority of Hong Kong's 6 mn population, swelled by refugees from the mainland, is intensely capitalist and has brought pressure to bear for democratic reforms that would allow the territory's affairs to be run by local people before and, hopefully, after the proper transfer of sovereignty. The Chinese government, on the other hand, would like the Hong Kong government, which is still ruled by Westminster, to halt all political reforms until 1990, when the so-called Basic Law would come into being.

The Basic Law is a mini-constitution for the future of Hong Kong Special Administrative Region or SAR drafted by Peking with the participation of 23 Hong Kong representatives. The foundation of the document, a blueprint of which is expected by 1987, is the 'one country two systems' principle, which ensures that Hong Kong's capitalist system will remain unchanged for fifty years following 1997. It will further define the relationship between the SAR and Peking, but will not necessarily define in detail how Hong Kong's internal affairs will be conducted.

There is fear in Hong Kong that Britain, which does not wish to alienate the Chinese and has no real stakes now in Hong Kong's future, will function chiefly as a mouthpiece for Peking, and Peking will bypass the electoral system with a bureaucracy of 'consultants'. The British are urging the Hong Kong people to express their views and fend for themselves.

China's position is that the British should maintain the status quo until 1997. The Chinese do not want to confront a situation in which the British can disclaim responsibility and say they can no longer influence local legislation such as the Legislative Council or Legco which is Hong Kong's lawmaking advisory body, or the Basic Law Consultative Committee (BLACC) for collecting opinion on the mini-constitution. Peking's ultimate fear is that Hong Kong will become so independent that when 1997 rolls around, it will not want to be returned to China.

Politics has played a backstage role to date in Hong Kong life: in fact, a low degree of confrontation has always been cited as a leading factor in Hong Kong's success. The highest policy-making body, the Executive Council or Exco, is staffed with government-appointed lay advisors called 'unofficials'. These advisors are known collectively as Umelco, are appointed on their own merits and are accountable only to the governor. At present there are 34 of them. Their number is split between members of the old boys' club, whose main concern is to avoid political polarisation, and ambitious new blood seeking positioning in the future government.

The local wealthy Chinese are forming a faction of their own, known as the Progressive Hong Kong Society, or PHS, which is backed by a number of business concerns.

31

Economic scene

Hong Kong is the world's 15th-largest exporter. The tiny nation leads the world, in absolute value terms, in exports of clothing, fur and garments, toys, artificial flowers and candles. In terms of volume, it also leads in exports of watches, radio-receivers and clocks. It is also a major services centre offering financial, trade and shipping services.

Like the other NICs, Hong Kong has been hard hit by protectionism and by the world recession. Its leading export, textiles, is its most vulnerable. A steady stream of 'calls' by the United States against textiles and garment exports has made almost 90% of the territory's exports subject to quota limits. Country-of-origin legislation imposed unilaterally this year brought an end to subassembly work in mainland China and forced exporters to invest heavily in high-technology Japanese knitting machinery.

Although Hong Kong still leads the world in textile exports, exports earnings fell 10% in 1985 (admittedly after a 25% rise in 1983 and a 38% rise in 1984). Real GDP increased by 8% from the previous year. GNP rose by 4.5% in 1985, with private investment going up while public investment dropped. Wages rose by 8% with inflation hovering at 7%, giving a slight boost to consumer spending.

Hong Kong has been revived as an entrepôt for mainland China, as China itself undergoes massive political, economic and social change.

Hong Kong is essential to China, especially as its own markets open up to the western world, both as a financial centre earning foreign exchange for the mainland and also because of the critical importance of its manufacturing sector. China is already taking steps to ensure its control of those assets and to erode the colonial legacy of the British in Hong Kong.

V South Korea

Political scene

Many Asia hands believe that South Korea holds out the most hope for the establishment of democratic constitutions in Asia today. Under Japanese occupation from 1910 when the Yi dynasty was abolished to 1945 when the country was liberated by US and Soviet forces, the country suffered a systematic humiliation. Today, it is Japan's most ardent competitor in the Pacific Basin and is striving to be recognised as a western, 'progressive' country.

The current constitution, the 'Yushin' or Revitalising Constitution of 1972 which inaugurated the Fourth Korean Republic, is authoritarian and anti-democratic and is basically a self-serving document legitimising the rule of President Chun Doo Hwan. It defines the president's role as that of a supreme and benevolent dictator above political strife. The president is indirectly elected by an electoral college, called the National Conference for Unification, for a term of six years with no limit on re-election. Barring voluntary retirement, a president could remain in power for life. He has broad discretionary powers during periods of national emergency, including the temporary suspension of the basic rights of the people and the issuance of decisions and ordinances that may not be challenged or subjected to judicial review. He is also empowered to appoint members of the judiciary at all levels and to discipline them for misconduct. In addition to being the chief executive, the president is also the Head of the National Security Council, Chairman of the State Council and the National Conference for Unification, and Commander-in-Chief of the armed forces.

The State Council functions as the cabinet. Its membership is neatly circular, including the president as chairman, and at least 15 ministers. The prime minister and ministers are appointed by the president and are responsible collectively and individually to him. President Chun Doo Hwan, who took power by military coup after the assassination of President Park Chung Hee in 1978, has introduced some liberalising reforms. Soon after his accession, he initiated a new constitutional referendum which reduces the presidential powers. While some of these may be as self-serving as the Yushin Constitution itself, the president can no longer appoint one-third of the National Assembly or name judges. He is himself limited in tenure to one seven-year term. Human rights and habeas corpus have been guaranteed and forcible extraction of confession from political prisoners is forbidden.

33

Dogged by scandals which touched his own family, Chun also waged war against government corruption and inefficiency. Nearly 8,667 public servants, journalists, teachers and politicians were purged including 232 senior ministers and 431 officials of state-controlled banks and corporations. The opposition leader Kim Dae Jung and 23 of his supporters were also indicted on charges of violating national security laws and plotting insurrection. Chun relaxed press censorship in early 1980 and restored political rights to Kim and others. But, following student riots in Seoul and Kwangju, the government rationalised a heavy-handed military response that claimed hundreds of lives. The government also rearrested Kim, who fled to asylum in America. His sentence was later suspended.

Kim returned to South Korea in 1985 to lead his party, the New Korea Democratic Party or NKDP, in a drive to change the constitution to allow direct presidential elections to replace the electoral college system which he says favours the President's Democratic Justice party. Chun has pledged to leave office in 1988, but his opposition to the campaign for direct election indicates that he doubts a government party candidate would prevail in a fair election. He wants to delay constitutional revisions until 1989, saying that this would cause unrest when the nation must present a united front for the Olympic Games.

Economic scene

South Korea has often been referred to as 'Japan No. 2' in the Asian constellation. This bustling nation has developed many of the same trade relationships through keen competition with its industrious neighbour.

South Korean production of cars and sophisticated consumer electronic goods is already threatening to undercut Japan's position in the US export market, a prospect which staggers Americans who remember the devastation of Seoul, the Asian nation's capital and site of the 1988 Olympics, almost a decade after Japan had begun its famous recovery from World War II.

Since the Korean War, South Korea has developed with comparable speed. Like Japan, it has a highly-educated population, driven by the Confucian work ethic, which in thirty years has grown to 41 mn, as large as that of several major European nations. South

Korea has a gross national output of $81 bn, larger than that of half the members of the OECD. South Korea's raw industrial muscle has pushed it ahead of Austria, Belgium, Greece and Norway, and it is closing in on Sweden.

It has become America's seventh-largest trading partner, larger than France. In fact, it is the world's fourteenth-largest trader. South Korea's hosting of the 1988 Olympics is a sign of economic coming-of-age, as it was for Los Angeles in 1984 and Tokyo in 1964. The country is already a prominent player in the steel, shipbuilding, construction and electronics export markets. South Korean companies such as Samsung and Lucky-Goldstar have beaten the Japanese in the US market by offering lower prices and longer guarantees for video-cassette recorders and colour televisions. In 1985 a successful computer product was the Leading Edge Model D, made by Daewoo Corp., which sold at half the price of an IBM PC.

South Korea's per capita income has risen from $89 to $2,000 in just twenty years, putting the country on a par with Portugal. Unlike Japan, which began its export drive in an era of expanding world trade, South Korea is running headlong into the worst resurgence of protectionism since the 1930s. The construction, textile and shipbuilding industries are already in crisis, and Europe and Japan are blocking goods with trade barriers. In line with the Reagan administration's get-tough trade policy, the United States has imposed quotas on many Korean goods and is hammering on the country to force open its highly-protected domestic market to US companies.

This rapid growth has created its own problems as well. A wide gap exists between the elite and the workers, few of whom can afford to buy the consumer goods they create. The result is a divided society which increasingly challenges the authoritarian rule of President Chun Doo Hwan, successor to the assassinated Park Chung Hee. Unlike Japan, the workers are increasingly aware of these disparities and have engineered massive and disruptive strikes such as the one at Daewoo Motors in 1985, which won workers a 12.1% wage hike and a 4.3% bonus increment in the largest labour-management confrontation in South Korea since 1980. Average 1985 wage increases in South Korea reached 10% or more, double the 5.2% target of the Korea Employers' Federation. If this trend continues, it could undermine South Korea's competitiveness in the

35

world market, a serious problem in the light of the country's current-account deficit, which totalled $45 bn in 1985. However, so far Chun and his ruling Democratic Justice Party (DJP) have taken a moderate line and in fact promised an easing of current labour laws because of the fear that a harsh government stance could produce a backlash, driving labour, student, and other dissident groups together and creating the climate for serious unrest.

In order to keep the economic miracle alive and make payments on its $45 bn foreign debt, Korea needs to grow by 7% a year. Not content with a mere five-year plan, the forward-looking South Koreans have drafted a 'Blueprint for Long-term National Development to 2000' published in 1985 by the Korea Development Institute (KDI). In 1985, South Korea almost achieved its growth targets. Wages rose by 10% while inflation only rose by 3.5%, with real GDP growth close to 6.5%, boosting consumer spending. However, the study pointed out, a comprehensive programme of political, social and financial reform is needed for this growth to continue. In order to achieve the goal of per capita income of US$ 5,103 by the turn of the century, South Korea will have to develop its own broad rural and urban markets for consumer durables. Liberal democracy must be firmly established along with an institutionalised means for the peaceful transfer of power. Greater local autonomy, stronger respect for the law, and an improved administrative mechanism are also seen as necessary to ensure maximum economic efficiency.

On the business front, the KDI study calls for further efforts to increase competition and to ease the concentration of wealth by the large conglomerates, known as chaebol. When South Korea began its economic takeoff in the early 1960s, Park Chung Hee's government turned to a handful of proven family entrepreneurs led by the Chungs of Hyundai, the Koos of Lucky-Goldstar, the Lees of Samsung, and the Kims of Daewoo. Backed by massive amounts of low-cost funds, they built the chaebol on foreign investment and overseas borrowing. But their huge backlog of debt and inefficiencies has become a drag on the economy, while the concentration of vast wealth is a volatile political issue.

In 1984, the combined sales of South Korea's top 30 chaebol equalled three-quarters of the country's output of goods and services for that year while their debt equalled 48% of the country's total bank credits. The top twelve chaebol control virtually every aspect of South Korea's economy and have squeezed small and medium-sized business out of the market. Sales from the top four—Hyundai, Samsung, Lucky-Goldstar and Daewoo—equal 45% of the GNP.

However, as with Japan and the other NICs, South Korea has been hard hit by protectionism and in order to avoid this, companies have in the past kept their brand names as invisible as possible, selling under the labels of such US companies as RCA and GTE. Millions of Americans have purchased Korean goods without knowing or caring where they were made.

However, another problem associated with South Korean exports is the lack of a large domestic market which makes Korean product-testing inferior to the Japanese. Despite this the South Koreans have been able to capture market niches, for example in the automobile sector. Japan has effectively conceded the low end of the market to Korean cars. Toyota, Nissan and Honda have already moved upmarket to build bigger, more luxurious cars, the Japanese equivalent of the Mercedes. However, the Japanese are digging in in some areas such as semiconductors, where they have underpriced their products so drastically that the South Koreans can't manufacture them except at a loss.

Experts predict that, in the long run, economic pressures such as the rising value of the yen will continue forcing the Japanese upmarket, allowing the South Koreans to take over less expensive goods. However, some struggle can be expected as the Japanese are apt to retaliate if the South Koreans move in too fast. South Korea is compromised by its reliance on Japanese technology: more than 30% of money earned from selling Korean VCRs in the US, for example, goes to Japan to pay for parts South Korea cannot manufacture.

Lack of technology is South Korea's Achilles heel. So far the country has competed against Japan and the United States largely on the basis of labour costs. However, how long can this last, particularly with even cheaper labour just around the corner in China, and Korean workers' likely future demands for higher pay as the nation reaps the benefits of its export offensive? To help companies boost their high-tech expertise, the government is encouraging research, development and training with massive funding over the next five years, when the country plans to double its crop of engineers.

VI Singapore

Political scene

Singapore was an almost uninhabited island when Sir Stamford Raffles established a trading station of the British East India Company there in 1819. Five years later the island was ceded outright to the company by the Sultan of Jahore and was incorporated with Malacca and Penang to form the Straits Settlements, from which it was detached in 1946 to become a separate crown colony. In 1959 Singapore became a self-governing state and in 1963 it joined the new Federation of Malaysia. Singapore and Malaysia terminated the union in 1965, when the Republic of Singapore was proclaimed.

The legal basis of government is the charter called the Singapore Order of Council, 1958, under which Singapore becomes a self-governing colony. With some modification, this document became the constitution of the state of Singapore when it joined the Malaysia Federation in 1963. When Singapore left the Federation and declared its independence in 1965, it served as a framework for the new republic.

In form, the structure of government established by the constitution is parliamentary, but in substance and practice Singapore is an authoritarian and paternalistic state in which opposition is barely tolerated and in which the People's Action Party (PAP) has assumed a pre-emptive role. Because of the country's small size, the government, headed and personified by Prime Minister Lee Kuan Yew, exercises a direct and powerful influence on every aspect of political, economic and social life. Lee has presided over the economic miracle of Singapore for 31 years and his overriding concern is with efficiency and uninterrupted economic growth: the successful pursuit of these goals has resulted in a concentration of power in the bureaucracy and in an attrition of legislative powers and competitive politics.

In 1967, at the age of 43, Lee announced he was grooming an 'unending stream of people with character' to replace himself and Singapore's first generation of political leaders. Latterly, the chief contender for Lee's position has been his 34-year-old son, Lee Hsien Loong, a former brigadier general, scholar and charismatic politician whom observers say is a worthy successor to his father. However, Lee senior shows no signs of leaving yet: although he announced his departure in 1984 he remained in office to see Singapore through its current economic crisis. He has indicated that he will stay only one more term.

Economic scene

In 1984, Singapore celebrated 25 years of self-rule during which the tiny country of 2.5 mn had prospered beyond its wildest dreams. Over those years it had done battle with communism, confronted Indonesia over that country's aborted fusion with Malaysia, and seen the slow submersion of its own ethnic, racial and religious differences beneath the emerging Singaporean national identity. It had seen the end of unemployment, bad housing and illiteracy. By exploiting its position on the Pacific trade routes, and by creating an efficient infrastructure of airport, seaport and telecommunication links, it had created a business environment which had attracted huge foreign investment. Per capita income stood at $6,000, as high as Italy's. The currency was one of the strongest in the world, with reserves of over US$ 10 bn. The benevolent strong-arm paternalism of Prime Minister Lee Kuan Yew and his government had created stability and continuity, and Lee was preparing to hand the reins to a successor. Real GNP growth was 9% compared to 7.9% in 1983.

In 1985 there was a turnaround. A sharp downturn in the long boom was accompanied by a stock market crash initiated by the collapse of the Pan-Electric group, one of Singapore's largest conglomerates. GDP, which rests on an economy whose main sectors are construction, trade, tourism, manufacturing, financial and business services, and transport and communication, sank 1.7%.

All of the NICs suffered to some extent in 1985, but Singapore was hardest-hit although it outperformed all the others in the recessions of 1973 and 1978–79.

Singapore's products have become no longer competitive in the world market. This has been due to several factors. Among them are government intervention through dramatic increases in the Central Provident Fund or CPF, a retirement scheme to which all employees contribute 25% of their earnings; a high-wage policy initiated in 1978–81 which fixed wages above market-clearing levels; and the heavy gambling of public investment in shipbuilding and petrochemicals with disastrous results.

A too-rapid shift in industrial gears may have had some effect as well. When labour-intensive industries were phased out, the new capital- and skill-intensive industries such as machinery, aerospace, computers, etc. couldn't rise up fast enough. Some light industry moved to Malaysia, and some was liquidated.

Another factor has been Indonesia's and Malaysia's nationalistic policies. Their direct trade has considerably reduced Singapore's entrepôt business. Also the high exit tax introduced by Indonesia has reduced Indonesia's tourism to Singapore and diminished its role as a medical centre.

In the long run, Singapore's physical and financial infrastructure is too strong to allow a permanent slide. However, the country will have to take certain restructuring measures. These are: to continue the upward shift of the industrial structure to the high-tech level because over the long run Singapore can't compete effectively with other countries with large labour forces and lower wages in the labour-intensive industries; to lower costs and increase productivity through various bonus or productivity incentives and new collective agreements; to review the overall tax system to reduce the tax burden of businesses so that they can compete more effectively (the current corporation tax rate in Singapore is 40%, whereas it is 17.5% in Hong Kong); to enhance entrepôt trade between China and Taiwan; and to reduce the CPF over the next two years, a scheme recently announced by Prime Minister Lee.

VII   Taiwan

Like the other NICs, cheap labour-dependent industries brought Taiwan rapid economic development in the 1960s and 1970s. Now, in the 1980s, it is facing a drop in world demand, steep competition from China, the ASEAN nations and other developing countries, and protectionist pressures from the US.

1985 witnessed a heavy brake on the Taiwanese economy, chiefly due to the disappointing trade performance. Real economic growth hovered at 4.8%, the lowest since 1982 when the economy expanded only 3.3%. Total foreign trade amounted to US$ 42.15 bn in the first ten months of the year, down 4% from the previous year. Exports declined marginally to US$ 25.5 bn during the same period, while imports dropped 8.6% to US$ 16.7 bn, bringing the current-accounts surplus close to US$ 10 bn. Approximately US$ 8.4 bn resulted from trade with the United States at levels virtually the same as 1984. On the other hand, Taiwan's trade deficit with Japan, its biggest supplier, dropped 32% from 1984 levels, to US$ 1.81 bn.

Although the drop in exports, if continued, might be expected to relieve the trade surplus, the sharper decline in imports has actually worsened it. Taiwan's foreign exchange reserves, held at the Central Bank of China, continue to mount rapidly. In 1985 they stood at a record US$ 21 bn compared to US$ 16.1 bn in 1984. Banking authorities say the majority is held in US Treasury bonds which have appreciated substantially as US interest rates have fallen.

The large foreign reserves threaten to exacerbate political friction with the United States over the continuing trade surplus. Also they have tended to create strong inflationary pressures. So far the monetary authorities have successfully combated the threat of inflation by issuing treasury bonds which soak up excess export earnings.

Perhaps most important, the existence of the reserves points out Taiwan's failure to utilise productively its massive capital. 1985 marked the fourth successive year of declining domestic capital investment. Politicians from the ruling Nationalist Party or Kuomintang have called on the government to use some of the reserves for domestic economic construction. Government forecasts for 1986 predict that its capital investment will rise 13%, mostly for infrastructure projects such as the so-called 14 Major projects which include harbour, rail, highway and energy development. A further acceleration of this rate could provide immediate stimulus to the flagging economy.

Another approach, favoured by development specialists, would be to upgrade the technological level of the island's industry. For the past five years the government has promoted this move as a priority. However, real progress has been slow. Specialists feel that the process could be speeded up if the government provided greater financial incentives to companies to make the necessary investments in new technologies; or if it funded research for engineers, computer scientists, and others of its highly-skilled citizens now working abroad. Another possibility would be for the government to provide companies interested in overseas investment with financial support, perhaps by setting up public-private ventures in specified areas.

The reciprocal of this plan, foreign and overseas Chinese investment in Taiwan, rose sharply in 1985. In the first ten months of that year, approved foreign investment, led by the United States and Japan, rose 39% to US$ 508 mn. The lion's share went into chemicals and pharmaceuticals production facilities, while machines and instruments manufacture absorbed 17%. The electronics and electric supply industries accounted for 15%.

So far the Kuomintang government has smoothly ridden over a crisis in confidence precipitated by the economic downturn and 18 months of scandals including the Cathay financial scandal which erupted in February 1985 around banking procedures in a major business group controlled by the Kuomintang, the 1984 murder of Kuomintang critic Henry Liu in America, and a series of bad industrial accidents and food-safety abuses. In a recent election the Kuomintang, headed by President Chiang Chin Kuo (Chiang Kai-Shek's son, popularly referred to as the 'Teflon Buddha') held on to 70% of the popular vote. Part of this may be due to the fact that television and newspapers are either government-controlled or heavily influenced by the government: allegations of cheating surfaced during the elections but were promptly and firmly squelched.

However, it is unlikely that political change will create the conditions for a change in economic policy in Taiwan. Elections are conducted under ground rules which heavily favour the ruling party. In contrast to the Kuomintang's year-round, tight-knit organisation, the opposition is not allowed to establish a formal party. Campaigns are legally limited to a short duration, which in addition to the media control makes it difficult for the opposition to get its views known. In addition, continuing ideological and personal splits within the opposition have led many people to question whether it is in fact a viable alternative to the Kuomintang.

The most radical changes that Taiwan can expect in the near future are some sort of readjustment, either by fiscal or monetary policy, to get the trade surplus under control; a further lowering of tariffs to stimulate imports and decrease protectionist pressures from the United States, and a significant appreciation in the New Taiwan dollar.

VIII   The primary commodity exporters—overview

The group of Pacific Basin economies which relies more on raw materials than on processed and manufactured goods as their engine of growth has faced its own set of problems in recent years. For Indonesia, an OPEC member, the collapse of crude oil prices has precipitated a number of grave macroeconomic policy problems. For Malaysia and the Philippines the general downward drift of the raw materials prices over the past six to ten years has eroded the purchasing power of many groups in the economy. These difficulties are being faced at the same time as efforts are being made to push towards industrialisation, often based on indigenous, raw materials processing.

IX   Indonesia

Political scene

Indonesia was the country most considered as a military fallback by the United States in the event of a political collapse in the Philippines. With Malaysia, Indonesia controls the Malacca Straits, a vital strategic and trade position. Leadership in both Malaysia and Indonesia believe that the bond between them, which is based on geographical proximity, similar ethnic identities, and a shared cultural heritage, has done much to guarantee peace in non-Communist Southeast Asia since the 1960s. The 1963 creation of a Malaysian Federation embracing Singapore, Sabah and Sarawak led to a violent three-year confrontation or 'Konfrontasi' between

Indonesia and Malaysia that 20 years later still stirs up old animosities.

Today, Indonesia is a far less democratic country than Malaysia, with a political tradition of consensus rather than parliamentary confrontation, and an enormous military influence in both political and commercial affairs. It has the worst record of human rights abuses in the world.

Indonesia has a unitary presidential government of 27 provinces with a strong republican tradition following years of struggle for independence from Dutch rule which ended in 1949. Relations between the two countries were seriously strained by Sukarno's expulsion of the Dutch, but are cordial today.

The government of Indonesia is based on a short, broadly-phrased constitution drafted in 1945 that defines the state ideology, Pancasila, as belief in one supreme god, a just and civilised humanity, nationalism, democracy, and social justice. It is deliberately secular to accommodate the 10% of Indonesians who are not Muslim.

The constitution provides for a strong executive form of government vesting all real power in the president. The supreme parliamentary body is the Madjelis Permusjwaratan Rakjat, or MPR, otherwise known as the People's Consultative Assembly. In theory this is superior to all other state entities including the presidency and the Supreme Court, which is only nominally independent of the president. The principal legislative body is the Dewan Perwakilan Rakjat (DPR).

When President Suharto launched his new order in 1967, he retained the basic features of the 1945 constitution, but incorporated them into a new power structure dominated by military generals and civilian technocrats. The power elite is composed of the Badan Kordinasi Intelidgen Negara or BAKIN, otherwise known as the State Intelligence Co-ordinating Board, the Kamando Operasi Permulskan Keamanan dan Ketertiban or the Command for the Restoration of Security and Order (KAMTIB), the Msujwarat Pimpinan Doerah or Regional Leadership Council (MUSPIDA).

Part of the reason for the military build-up is the ever-present threat of Islamic insurgence which is far more severe than in Malaysia.

The president is the chief executive and supreme commander of the armed forces. He is elected indirectly for a term of five years by the MPR and may stand for re-election any number of times. During the three decades of independence, Indonesia has had only four elections, two in 1955, one in 1971 and one in 1977.

Suharto, whose term of office expires in 1988, likes to be known as the 'father of Indonesian development'. He will almost certainly try to stay in office into the 1990s, ostensibly to see the country through the current economic downturn, caused by the collapse of oil and gas prices, which caused Suharto to initiate a radical spending cut.

Economic scene

Indonesia, the world's fifth most populous nation, is in serious economic difficulties, with no immediate signs of recovery. Faced with shrinking oil and gas revenues that account for 60% of the state budget and 70% of export earnings, it has slashed spending for the fourth year running.

The oil boom created immense change in this country of 155.7 mn inhabitants in the 1970s. Billions were spent on development, fortunes made, and foreign companies, led by Americans and Japanese, cashed in on the bonanza. Rich Indonesians became citizens of the world shopping-mall culture in Singapore, Paris and Hong Kong.

However this has all come to an end. Economic growth, forecast at 5% in 1985, dropped to 3% in that year and is still falling. The problem has been compounded by the poor performance of Indonesia's non-oil exports, which include coffee, rubber and palm oil. With the exception of coffee, world commodity prices remain depressed in all these areas.

Indonesia's small but hopeful industrial sector is in a tailspin, with many companies operating below capacity and a record number of bankruptcies. Japanese companies, hitherto the largest investors in

45

Indonesia, concede that more than 40% of their ventures are losing money.

Other factors in the reversal of the national fortunes include the continued slowdown in the world's economy, the adverse effect of protectionism on Indonesia's already battered textile sector, and increased debt repayments (Indonesia's foreign debt now equals US$ 27 bn).

The effect of this turnaround is the shelving of President Suharto's five-year plan, which was designed to lead Indonesia to 'economic takeoff' in the 1990s.

Indonesia has no foreign currency control, and the large capital outflows plus sharp drops in foreign and domestic investment augur even slower growth for the years ahead.

In order to cushion the effects of declining oil revenues Indonesia is diversifying into tree crops. The country has cheap and abundant labour and good plantation sites, in its outer islands. One of its neighbours, land-short and labour-starved Malaysia, is gradually abandoning rubber and oil palm tree crop production, potentially giving Indonesia virtually assured world leadership in those areas by the end of the century.

However, success is by no means assured. In part it depends on the future of Jakarta's ambitious Nucleus Estate and Smallholder (NES) scheme, a massive resettlement-cum-plantation development patterned after Malaysia's two decades-old Federal Land Development Authority Project (FELDA). But Indonesia's sheer size and diversity, along with other factors such as a large and inert bureaucracy, make FELDA difficult to evaluate. As a result, industry sources feel Indonesia will be lucky to achieve even 60% of the 1.2 mn new plantation developments earmarked under the current five-year plan.

In addition, the country must devise some way to deal with poor labour utilisation, inferior quality control, and unwieldy and bureaucratic marketing procedures. If it does so, it will be in a better position to maintain export market shares.

In an effort to balance the 1986 budget Saharto has announced a 7% spending cut from 1985 levels. This will bring 1986 spending to $19.1 bn, the first decline in 14 years. Development spending will suffer most, with a slash of 22% and no new projects for 1986–87. Debt repayment, up 18.7%, will become the biggest component (almost one-third) of the government's recurrent expenditure. The current-account deficit is expected to slide marginally, to $2.2 bn.

Suharto has ruled out a devaluation of the rupiah, which has been a source of continuing speculation as oil prices weaken. He has targeted as long-range goals a need to increase state revenues for domestic resources and to make development spending more efficient. In addition, the liberalised banking sector is expected to mobilise more funds.

X Malaysia

Political scene

Politics in Malaysia represent not so much a secular ideology as a series of fragmented ethnic, religious and linguistic constituencies, and not so much a link between government and people as a relic of the old Asian village system.

The ethnic composition of the population falls into two main categories: native tribal groups such as the Sea Dayaks or original headhunters of Borneo, the Chinese, the Indians, and the indigenous Malays or Bumiputras whose interests have been built into the constitution by Prime Minister Mahathir Mohamed and have been further reinforced by the establishment of Islam as the national religion and Malay as the national language.

The offices of the yang di-pertuan agong (the Malaysian head of state) and the prime minister are open only to a Malay. The structure of the federal parliament favours Malay membership as well.

Until recently, the Chinese, who are the second-largest ethnic group and who also dominate the economy, have been indifferent to politics and excluded from government. Unfortunately, the Malaysian-Chinese Association, the most influential Chinese party in

47

Malaysia and a member of the National Front Coalition now in power, has been discredited by the involvement of its president, Tan Koon Swan, in the failure of Pan-Electric Industries, a large Singapore conglomerate whose collapse caused the unprecedented failure of the Singapore and Kuala Lumpur Stock Exchange.

The fourth major group, the Indians, comprise Pakistanis, Sri Lankans and Indians proper, and make up about 10% of the population.

The government of Malaysia is based on the constitution of 1957 as amended to accommodate the special interests of Sabah and Sarawak, which joined the federation in 1963. It established a federal system of government under a constitutional monarchy of 13 federated states (including nine headed by sultans).

Malaysia observes parliamentary norms far more closely than its neighbour, Indonesia. It has a unique 'revolving kingship' system for re-electing the titular head-of-state for a five-year term, and a large religious bureaucracy reinforcing royal prerogatives in determining proper Islamic conduct and ritual. The supreme head of the federation is the yang di-pertuan agong, who is elected for five years by and from the conference of rulers, the majlis raja-raja. Executive power is vested in a prime minister and cabinet responsible to a bicameral legislature consisting of a partially-appointed senate and an elected house of representatives. The administration is strongly centralised. The federal parliament has sole authority to legislate in the fields of external affairs, defence, internal security, justice, citizenship (except in Sabah and Sarawak), industry, commerce, finance, communication, transportation and education.

Malaysia considers itself non-aligned, and is a member of the non-aligned Afro-Asian group of nations at the United Nations. In an effort to make wider diplomatic contacts, ties have been established with the Soviet Union, the People's Republic of China, the Eastern European Soviet bloc, North Korea and Vietnam.

Regional consideration co-operation is central to Malaysian foreign policy, and Malaysia has played an active role in ASEAN since 1967, when that organisation was first formed. Relations with Singapore, strained by that country's withdrawal from the Malaysian federation in 1965, have improved considerably in recent years. Ties with the Philippines continue to be eroded by territorial disputes over the Philippines' claim to Sabah and over Malaysian assistance to Moro rebels in Mindanao. A territorial rift also exists with Thailand over Thai claims to the Malay provinces of Kedah, Trengganu, Perlis and Kilantan, as well as Malaysian claims to the four southern Thai provinces which have Malay populations. In recent years these differences have diminished and Malaysia has pledged support to Thailand in the event of a Communist invasion.

Malaysia's political future is uncertain in the light of growing speculation regarding the tenure of Dr Mahathir, previously known for his staying power as well as for his tremendous self-confidence. He is facing many challenges: the testing of federal-state relations in Sabah, the instability of the opposition Parti Bersatsu Sabah which had the support of the Mahathir government, the growing belief that the federal parliament has become little more than a rubber stamp for pre-set policies, a constitutional row between Mahathir and hereditary sultans ruling nine of the thirteen states, and discredit from the various corruption scandals which have plagued his government.

Economic scene

Malaysia is a major world producer of five key commodities: rubber, palm oil, tin, timber and pepper; it is also a significant exporter of oil and gas. Until recently it has also enjoyed a strong, stable government and annual growth rates averaging 8.5%, with one of the world's strongest currencies, the ringgit.

However, like a number of other Pacific Basin countries, 1985 saw a sharp downturn for the once-thriving country. A series of shocks, including the familiar ones of recession and protectionism, but also the Singapore and Kuala Lumpur stock market crash of December 1985, labour unrest among government employees, and an unprecedented clash between government troops and Islamic fundamentalists, has shaken faith in the country's future, which is also still suffering the aftershocks of the Bumiputra Malaysia Finance corruption scandal in 1983. The GNP growth rate is expected to drop to 6% in 1986, and several economic observers doubt that even this can be achieved. Commodity prices have

49

dropped off drastically in the country's five key exports, and similarly oil prices have fallen considerably.

XI   The Philippines

Political scene

The revolution in the Philippines in early 1986 was only surprising in its bloodlessness. For the two decades that Ferdinand Marcos ruled the country, first as elected leader and then as corrupt dictator, the country which had been billed in the 1960s as East Asia's economic miracle slipped behind all of its neighbours in economic growth, stability, security and political maturity.

The Philippines was brought to boiling point by Marcos' failure to deliver on all fronts. Political institutions crumbled under the weight of his one-family rule and numerous hangers-on, added to that of a corrupt military correctly identified by the people as privileged tools of the President. The Philippines were cut out of the region's growth by remaining too dependent on volatile commodities pushed by Marcos' cronies. Foreign debt, inflation and corruption all contributed to the backward momentum.

When Corazon Aquino, widow of slain opposition leader Benigno Aquino, gained victory out of the February 7, 1986 election, it was due to her promise as a fresh start, her reputation as a straight-forward and principled person, and the support of the army, the Roman Catholic Church, the Philippine business community, and, finally, the United States, which all united behind her.

The constitution of 1973 masterminded by Marcos set up a titular president as head-of-state, elected for a six-year term by a majority of the National Assembly. The constitution also vested an array of broad powers in the office of the prime minister who was given control of executive departments and local governments, the function of commander-in-chief of the armed forces, and treaty authority, along with the power to impose martial law. 'Transitory provisions' allowed Marcos to hold the posts of both president and prime minister indefinitely.

Aquino's first measures included a review of the constitution, followed by elections for a new legislature and for thousands of municipal and provincial offices; an upending of the Marcos system of patronage and 'warlord' loyalists; mending a fractured economy, and a stemming of the Communist guerrilla war.

In the matter of foreign policy, Mrs Aquino's most important task will be to renegotiate a relationship with the United States. Many Filipinos feel let down at Washington's eleventh-hour repudiation of Marcos and President Reagan's statement that the Marcos-Aquino election was marred by fraud and violence on both sides. Anti-Americanism, unheard-of before the event, is now commonplace, and Filipinos are also unhappy at the suggestion that the CIA might in fact have scripted the ouster. If Aquino is to be perceived as her own person in politics, she will have to wean herself away from dependence on the US; and the US, in order to retain good feeling in the Philippines, will have to downplay the interventionist role it has hitherto pursued in the interests of protecting its massive defence installations at Subic Naval Base and Clark Air Base.

However, her principal problems have lain closer to home with the need to wrest political control. She removed her main threat in November 1986 when Defence Minister Juan Ponce Ennile was forced to resign and therefore reduced the immediate prospect of a coup and heightening political tensions. However, Ennile is believed to have considerable support among mid-level officers in the military and although 62 years of age he is unlikely to depart from the political scene despite professing to have little further active interest in government.

Economic scene

Aside from Singapore, the Philippines was the only Pacific Basin economy to show negative growth in 1985. Real GDP fell 4.5%, largely due to questions about the country's political future in the light of President Ferdinand Marcos' intentions and abilities, and the growing problem of insurgency. Overall investment declined for the second successive year, although not as sharply as in 1984, when it plunged 28%. Restrictive money policy drove interest rates high, while demand for the country's key exports, such as sugar, copper, textiles and semiconductors, remained weak. A decline in real wages was accompanied by a 20% hike in inflation; many agricultural workers, displaced because of the dismal performance of sugar and coconut exports, embraced communism for a promise of a better life and there was widespread labour unrest throughout the country.

Philippine businessmen attribute the current economic growth constraints to 'macro concerns' emanating from government conduct, government economic policies, bureaucracy and tariff rates. Chief among these concerns are continued heavy spending by the government on certain high-cost projects whose benefits are widely questioned, such as the huge financing requirements of the Philippine National Bank and the Development Bank of the Philippines. Both of these government-owned institutions are saddled with non-performing foreign currency loans. Efforts to merge the two to save on operating costs have been postponed indefinitely.

Currently, the Philippine money supply is guided by the conditions set by the IMF that accompany that agency's financial support to the official recovery programme which is aimed at correcting the imbalance that arose from overdependence on short-term foreign borrowing, high interest rates and weak export prices. This programme has the support of the IMF in the form of a standby credit facility equivalent to US$ 666.1 mn.

However, the business community feels that the recovery programme is penalising the wrong sector. A study published by the state-run University of the Philippines (UP) found that the private sector has shrunk proportionately faster, in terms of output and employment, than the public sector comprised of government and quasi-government enterprises. Overall, the study found the economy has contracted by 10% over the past ten years.

By shifting their focus to small, rural-based enterprises, Philippine businessmen are drifting further away from developing the spectrum of world-scale industries capable of earning the large export revenues needed to offset poor earnings from traditional exports.

XII Australia and New Zealand

While different from the Pacific Basin economies in many important respects—the dominance of Anglo-Saxon settlers, long-established trade and cultural ties with Europe, small and highly protected manufacturing sectors—these two countries are increasingly being drawn into the new pattern of intra-Pacific trade. One force, that of Japanese investment in Australian manufacturing capacity, is drawing Australia into the complex out-sourcing and sub-assembly fronts which seem likely to be important facets of Pacific Basin manufacturing in the next decade. Another factor is the increasing interest of Asian countries in drawing on the expertise of Australia and New Zealand in agriculture. Many of the Pacific Basin countries are at that stage of development where basic dietary needs have been met, by and large, and the next push is into more meat consumption and into more processed foods in general. This could be an important new source of interaction between the region's members.

Australian and New Zealand politics are most like those of the mother-country, Great Britain, as both countries were settled as penal colonies in 1788 and 1769 respectively. Each has a governor-general reflecting the British sovereign, and a parliament consisting of a House of Representatives and a Legislative Council. Parliaments are elected through popular elections; the distribution of federal and state powers is similar to that of the United States and both countries are noted for their liberal legislation on such issues as women's rights, old-age and invalid pensions, and childbirth subsidies. Like Great Britain, both have highly-factionalised Labour governments.

In Australia the majority party is the Australian Labour Party, led by Prime Minister Bob Hawke, and in New Zealand there is also a Labour government, led by David Lange.

Australia

Over the past twenty years, the primary thrust of the Australian economy has been to overcome its traditional dependence on the United Kingdom as an export market. Prior to the UK's entry into the EEC, it was Australia's chief export market under the Commonwealth Preferred Agreement. However, when the UK entered the European Community, Australia, being a non-member, could no longer trade with it and was forced to develop other markets, primarily in the Middle East and Asian-Pacific area. Regarding the latter area Australia's resource richness is complementary. Australia possesses mineral wealth and produces hefty food supplies which are lacking in the northern Pacific Basin countries. Japan is the main importer of Australian exports with the US second and New Zealand third. Australian exports to Japan are largely raw materials while cars and electronic goods flow the other way.

However, Australia is running into competition from the United States in supplying beef and grain to countries such as Japan. The US farm protection bill signed by President Reagan in 1985 has been widely criticised in Australia as a means of following the EEC down the path of highly-subsidised agriculture which will have a severe impact on Australia as a smaller producer of temperate-zone commodities. A government study completed in 1985 said that depression of world prices by EEC policy costs Australia A$ 1 bn per year.

In 1985 the Australian dollar fell to a record low of 62.0 US cents. This in part reflected doubt that the government could control a current-accounts deficit which seemed to be heading towards A$ 11 bn from an earlier forecast of A$ 8.5 bn. Although the actual figure turned out closer to A$ 6.7 bn on total outlays of A$ 64 bn, the government took stringent action by spending cuts of more than A$ 1 bn and by levying a tax-reform which imposed a heavy burden on business. The corporate tax rate was raised from 46% to 49%, fringe benefits became taxable, and all income earned by Australian companies abroad became taxable at home.

Overall, the GDP levelled out between 3.5% and 4%. Investment slowed in both the public and the private sectors, with increasing conflicts in the ruling Labour Party factions and a general weakening of government-union relations.

The devaluation of the Australian dollar had significant beneficial effects however. International competitiveness improved and Australian exporters found that they could even compete with some price advantage in the Asian markets.

New Zealand

Like Australia, New Zealand's economy rides firmly on farming, with meat, wool and dairy products accounting for around half of New Zealand's merchandise exports.

New Zealand Finance Minister Roger Douglas has initiated a three-to-five-year programme to pull the country out of 30 years of low growth. The aim has been to sweep away the old structure with its controls and restrictions which were designed to protect domestic producers. The programme is composed of a package of measures which helps farmers to get off the land, lowers many tariffs and exposes New Zealand Steel to competition as part of a larger shake-up of state enterprise.

New Zealand's main trading partners are the US and Australia, although the country is working hard to develop trade links with Pacific Basin South American states such as Chile.

Chapter Three

COMMODITIES AND COMMODITY TRADE IN THE PACIFIC BASIN

I   Introduction

Although conventionally grouped together for purposes of broad brush economic forecasting, in fact primary commodities can and do show widely differing market trends, both between groupings such as energy and minerals, food, and non-food agricultural commodities and within these categories; for instance, in metals, between tin and copper or in food, between wheat and coffee. This heterogeneity is not surprising since commodity markets are affected not only by general economic factors such as real GNP growth, inflation and interest rates, but also by commodity specific trends such as harvests, successful and unsuccessful buffer stock activity, structural changes affecting consumption and production of particular commodities (such as changes in the prices of synthetic or recycled substitutes), and a variety of government policies. Nevertheless, despite such important differences, primary commodities do share two key characteristics distinguishing them from manufactured goods and services. First, much of world trade in commodities takes place on a 'flex-price' basis and indeed via highly-organised commodity exchanges, often with well-developed futures markets. Thus the amount and anticipated change in demand and supply are quickly reflected in price. Second, for most commodities, changes in stocks play a major role in determining market conditions. This is because output and consumption often show large fluctuations due to factors such as weather and the trade cycle but are themselves highly unresponsive to price changes in the short term, thus forcing stock movements to balance the market.

II   Pacific Basin commodities

This chapter will discuss non-energy commodity production and trade in the Pacific Basin; the next chapter will deal with energy in the region. Many of the Pacific Basin countries are either major producers of non-energy commodities, or play very important roles in world trade for commodities. Some countries are generally thought of as commodity producers and exporters, such as Australia, Indonesia, Malaysia, New Zealand and the Philippines, while others are either consumers or importers, such as Hong Kong, Japan, South Korea and Taiwan. Singapore, besides being a consumer of commodities itself, is a major 'entrepôt' and trading centre for some of the region's commodities, and particularly for those from Malaysia. Hong Kong is also an entrepôt, particularly for goods being traded with China (PRC), although most of these goods are manufactures rather than commodities.

Of course, following the principle of international specialisation and the logic of resource endowments, even the commodity exporters import some primary products. For example, Malaysia imports sugar while South Korea, a commodity importer, is a major exporter of tobacco and tungsten. Nevertheless, the broad distinction between those countries where commodities supply a major share of export income and those where commodities are thought of mainly in terms of imports is useful.

As Table 3.1 shows, non-energy commodities account for a significant proportion of total exports in the five countries that are classified as Pacific Basin commodity exporters. This is so even in nations like Indonesia and Malaysia where oil and gas exports are very important export products. It is interesting to note that commodity exports are of greatest relative importance to Australia and New Zealand, the most highly developed of the five.

TABLE 3.1   NON-ENERGY PRIMARY COMMODITY SHARE OF TOTAL EXPORTS, PACIFIC BASIN COMMODITY EXPORTERS, 1983/84

%	
Australia	41.1
Indonesia	14.2
Malaysia	37.6
New Zealand	58.6
Philippines	38.3
Average	38.0

Source: National Statistics

III   World commodity trade background

According to a World Bank study of trade of about 30 primary products, in the early 1980s non-petroleum commodity exports were valued at $140 bn, some 8% of total world exports. Until the recent collapse of world oil prices, primary product trade was less than half the value of oil exports, but at current low oil prices, non-oil commodities in aggregate will make up a bigger share of total world trade. The most important primary products from a worldwide perspective are shown in Table 3.2. There are 20 primary products whose trade is valued at about $2 bn or over, although the most important of these are timber, wheat, sugar, corn and coffee. Interestingly, of those five, only timber is a non-food item. Breaking down the products by type, among the top 20, there are 9 food items, 4 non-food agricultural products, 2 animal products, and 5 mineral products.

TABLE 3.2   MAJOR WORLD-WIDE NON-ENERGY COMMODITY EXPORTS

US$ mn			
Timber	17,989	Wool	3,860
Wheat	17,042	Rubber	3,412
Sugar	13,340	Tin	3,011
Corn	11,056	Hides/skins	2,443
Coffee	10,144		
Copper	9,040	Cocoa	2,349
Beef	8,351	Zinc	2,259
Cotton	7,183	Phosphate rock	2,018
Iron ore	6,705	Tea	1,829
Rice	4,978	Palm oil	1,808
Tobacco	4,276		

Source: World Bank

Some Pacific Basin countries are major suppliers of these commodities, such as Australia, Malaysia and Indonesia, and others, especially Japan, are major markets for them. The region's importance in the world supply of many of these commodities is shown in Table 3.3. However, the Pacific Basin countries are also important producers of other products such as aluminium, lead, zinc and tungsten as shown in Table 3.4. The region, though, is only a minor supplier of certain other key minerals, such as the chromite produced in the Philippines used to make chromium.

TABLE 3.3 PACIFIC BASIN NATIONS: SHARE OF SELECTED WORLD COMMODITY EXPORTS

Commodity	Countries	Combined share of world exports %
Wheat	Australia	11.5
Sugar	Philippines, Australia, South Korea	9.2
Timber	Indonesia, Malaysia, Philippines	18.2
Iron ore	Australia, Philippines	21.6
Bananas	Philippines	9.5
Coffee	Indonesia, Philippines	4.4
Rubber	Malaysia, Indonesia	73.0
Tin	Malaysia, Indonesia, Australia	46.0
Cocoa	Indonesia, Malaysia	3.9
Tea	Indonesia, Taiwan	6.0
Palm oil	Malaysia, Indonesia	73.0
Coconut oil	Philippines, Malaysia	77.1
Copper	Australia, Philippines	44.1
Cotton	Australia	4.0

Source: World Bank, US Bureau of Mines, US Dept of Agriculture

As Table 3.5 shows, on the demand side the Pacific Basin countries are also important consumers in the global context. With its large, resource-poor but rapidly growing economy, Japan is a major market for numerous products world-wide and particularly for mineral products and rubber that are used for electronic and machinery products. Interestingly, sugar, cocoa and cotton are the only three products whose consumption by the nine other Pacific Basin countries combined is greater than that of Japan's alone. This reflects the larger population of the nine, as well as the importance to them of cotton as an input into textiles, the most important industrial product of countries such as South Korea, Taiwan and Hong Kong. For many commodities especially important to Pacific Basin producers, such as tropical wood, rubber and iron ore, Japan is the largest importer or second-largest single consumer in the

TABLE 3.4 PACIFIC BASIN NATIONS: SHARE OF SELECTED WORLD COMMODITY OUTPUT

Early 1980s

Commodity	Countries	Combined share of world output %
Wool	Australia, New Zealand	41.3
Copper	Australia, Philippines	16.3
Lead	Australia	14.3
Zinc	Australia	11.0
Aluminium	Australia, Japan, Indonesia	6.0
Nickel	Australia, Indonesia, Philippines	21.4
Tungsten	South Korea, Australia	10.2
Cobalt	Australia	4.3
Chromite	Philippines	2.8

Source: US Bureau of Mines, US Dept of Agriculture

world. In some cases, it derives a large share of its imports from Pacific Basin suppliers. The rapidly-growing NICs are also increas-

TABLE 3.5 PACIFIC BASIN SHARE OF WORLD CONSUMPTION OF SELECTED COMMODITIES

% Commodity	Japan	Other nine	Total
Aluminium	11.6	3.3	14.9
Cocoa	2.1	4.1	6.2
Copper	13.7	3.8	17.5
Cotton	4.5	6.4	10.9
Lead	6.7	2.5	9.2
Nickel	17.0	0.6	17.6
Rubber	12.2	9.8	22.0
Sugar	3.0	6.1	9.1
Tin	14.4	4.9	19.3
Zinc	12.7	5.5	18.2

Source: Malaysian Rubber Bureau, US Bureau of Mines, US Dept of Agriculture

ingly important as markets for commodity exports produced within the region. In addition to cotton, they are important consumers of rubber and mineral products such as zinc, aluminum, copper and tin. Nevertheless, Japan clearly remains the dominant consuming nation in the region, as well as from the point of view of overall world trade in commodities.

IV Near-term perspectives

Looking first at the short term, on balance, 1985 was a year of soft markets and generally weak prices that were not usually offset by strong export volumes. Whether measured in terms of sterling, US dollars, or SDRs, in 1985, primary commodity indices were below 1984 levels for all food, non-food agricultural materials, and metals. *A fortiori,* in dollar and SDR terms, average commodity prices remained far below their 1980 peaks, though sharp declines in the pound since that time meant that commodity prices measured in terms of sterling were well above 1980 levels. However, for commodity producers in some countries, e.g. Australia, commodity prices in local currency terms rose in 1985 due to the devaluation of their local currencies against the strong dollar. Nevertheless, and recognising exceptions for some commodities like coffee, on an overall basis 1985 was not a year of strong performance on commodity markets.

While the likelihood is that the US dollar will continue to fall or at best stabilise against most other major trading currencies (and especially the yen), in general, commodity prices in 1986 seem unlikely to strengthen much, largely because of disappointing economic performance in the United States and several other major industrial countries. Also the fall in oil prices has caused governments like Indonesia and Malaysia to focus more on exporting non-energy commodities to generate cash flow and thereby risking price collapses by boosting export volume. However, the stabilising of oil prices towards the end of 1986 should ease the potential downward pressure on non-energy commodity prices.

V Long-term outlook

Without doubt, the most important single factor affecting Pacific

Basin commodity trade is OECD economic trends. Besides Japan, Australia and New Zealand, themselves OECD members, North America and western Europe are major importers of many Pacific Basin commodities and indirectly are important as major influences on the economies of other commodity importing countries within the Pacific Basin (as well as on other regions of the world, such as Latin America).

While the OECD countries seem unlikely to return to the halcyon days of high growth and low inflation preceding the first oil shock, there is good reason to believe that OECD economic expansion in the next few years will be noticeably faster than in the last dozen years, thus raising commodity demand. Whether or not OPEC succeeds in achieving an agreement that restores some control over oil markets, oil prices are likely to average well below their 1980–1984 levels. Most observers believe that, despite serious problems for oil-producing countries and those countries which supply them, the net effect of the oil price drop will be to boost growth prospects in heavily import dependent countries in the Pacific Basin such as Japan and Korea, and outside it, in most of western Europe.

One of the key links between lower oil prices and faster growth is lower inflation leading to lower interest rates. While lower expectations of inflation would tend to weaken commodity demand by encouraging de-stocking, lower interest rates operate in the opposite direction. On balance, the net effect of lower oil prices and faster growth is stronger commodity demand.

VI Structural change

In the industrial countries in recent years, many observers have focused their economic analysis on factors decoupling the relationship between economic growth and commodity demand. The decline in the basic materials-intensity of GNP has been evident. Examples include the decreased use of metals due to the miniaturisation of many products and the substitution of plastics or other man-made materials for minerals. The supposed decline of manufacturing in the industrial countries is also often cited as a factor holding down the demand for primary products. Some aspects of these trends, such as the decline of manufacturing, are greatly exaggerated and others reflect not a decline in materials usage world-wide but its shift from traditional production centres to new locations. However, a number of Pacific Basin exporters of many industrial materials faces an ongoing problem of structural change reflecting the inexorable progress of science and technology in highly innovative free-market economies with the substitution of new materials for commodities, e.g. the displacement of sugar by high fructose corn syrup in many developed country markets. The phase-out of lead usage in petrol in the United States is another instance and is a reflection of a political choice emphasising environmental values over economic factors, i.e. the decline in commodity demand was unrelated to price which is invariably the driving force behind commodity substitution.

The Pacific Basin commodity-exporters are already well aware of the structural problems they face, as witnessed by their support of organisations such as the International Rubber Research Organisation, designed to strengthen demand for natural rubber by improving its qualities and finding new uses for it in order to retain and expand markets for rubber. Lower oil prices, by cutting the cost of feedstock for the production of many synthetic products, will have a major negative price impact on markets for many industrial materials. This, in turn, will certainly act as a price depressant for a number of commodities such as rubber. However, even here the downside effects must not be overblown. For instance, with current technology in the manufacturing of radial tyres, it is desirable to use natural rubber for 30% of it, and even radically-lower synthetic prices will not cause a massive decline in this important natural rubber market.

Furthermore, in certain cases synthetics seem unable to compete on quality grounds with natural commodities, as for example, man-made fibres versus wool or even cotton or silk in clothing manufacture. While in the near term, low synthetic prices may displace natural fibres, over the long term, countries such as Australia and New Zealand are likely successfully to outcompete synthetics in terms of price. The faster that GNP and consumer incomes grow in the wealthy countries, the greater will be the competitive strength of natural fibres *vis-à-vis* the less desirable synthetics. Given the opportunities presented by economic growth and consumer preference, the position of Pacific Basin exporters of wool and cotton, like many other commodities, will depend on marketing and support of research to ensure that the use of wool and cotton remains compatible with changing consumer preferences in areas such as clothing.

VII Competitiveness

Given overall commodity demand trends, the strength of the markets facing Pacific Basin exporters, in particular, will depend on their competitiveness *vis-à-vis* suppliers in the rest of the world such as other commodity exporting countries and domestic producers in importing countries. The relative competitive strength of Pacific Basin exporters depends in varying degrees on their own policies and on policies followed by other countries.

Within the region, Japan's import policies are clearly very important, and the commodity exporters would certainly benefit from much greater liberalisation in many areas, providing, of course, that reductions in trade barriers are not shaped so as to limit increased access mainly to US goods. Given continuing trade friction between Washington and Tokyo, the Pacific Basin commodity exporters will have to remain alert to the risk that any freeing of Japanese trade will involve *de facto* discrimination in favour of the United States and against the region's exporters. Such discrimination could mean lessened access to the Japanese market for the region's commodity exporters, despite the obvious locational advantages.

Outside of the region, the risk of reduced access for Pacific Basin exports of industrial raw materials seems very limited, particularly with regard to the United States market. President Reagan has resisted strong political pressures and International Trade Commission (i.e. the former Tariff Commission) recommendations to restrict copper imports. Nor does it now seem likely that any Canada-United States free trade agreement will favour mineral imports from Canada over those from the Pacific Basin countries. Thus, while exporters to the United States will have to contend with a somewhat stronger anti-dumping enforcement, existing trade is unlikely to be curtailed significantly. The United States Government, at least for the moment, seems likely to let US domestic minerals production shrink further if it cannot meet competition from abroad, so imports could even rise if structural change and competition from the exporting countries permit.

In contrast, on the agricultural side, United States trade policies like those of the EEC nations are likely to remain highly restrictive, greatly limiting access to US and European markets for Pacific Basin agricultural exports such as wheat, dairy products and meat. Further, the United States and the EEC will continue to stimulate exports artificially to third country markets which otherwise could be supplied by Pacific Basin nations such as Australia. In the case of sugar, Australia and the Philippines benefit from being able to sell certain limited quota volumes to the United States at the artificially high US price, but their limited gains are clearly far outweighed by the high degree of protectionism and trade distortion characteristic of the agricultural policies in the industrial world.

However, the US is more committed than most to free market trade although the recent US farm legislation (i.e. the Food Security Act of 1985) does not move the United States in a genuine free trade direction but simply increases that country's ability to compete on world markets. While this increased US competitiveness might eventually bring the EEC to the point of moderating its aggressive export subsidisation, this is far from certain. On balance, therefore, the new US farm law probably worsens the outlook for Pacific Basin agricultural exporters. Nor are there any signs of real change in the EEC, especially in view of continuing French pressures for very high farm support prices. Indeed, overall, the most feasible objective for Pacific Basin agricultural commodity exporters will be damage limitation rather than achieving substantial reduction in trade barriers or subsidies in the United States or Europe. For commodity importers, of course, US policies offer the possibility of lower import costs for products such as cotton.

Another important factor in determining competitiveness is exchange rates. The importance of currency management in maintaining the region's competitive position cannot be overstated. While individual countries may have kept their currencies overvalued for some periods, most have been willing to devalue when the need became apparent. Given the massive decline in oil export revenues, countries like Indonesia and Malaysia now may be motivated to devalue their currencies. The danger is that exchange rates may be set at levels which encourage excessive exports of commodities, thus depressing prices and export earnings.

A similar excess supply problem could also result from competition between the Pacific Basin and other exporting countries, or in some cases, between the Pacific Basin countries themselves. Of course, the notion of excessive competition in this context implies pure inelastic demand, but despite long-run substitution possibilities, this is not unrealistic from a short-term point of view. From an overall perspective, it is likely that for many commodities exported by the Pacific Basin nations, even with reasonably satisfactory OECD growth, there may be a tendency toward excess supply manifest by generally flat prices (measured in terms of some monetary unit such as the SDR which dampens the effect of individual currency fluctuations). There will be exceptions for individual commodities for certain periods of time, e.g. the near-term strong price outlook for coffee due to the poor weather in Brazil. However, by and large, Pacific Basin commodity producers will face fairly soft markets over the medium term. Certainly, there is little likelihood that more numerous or more effective international commodity agreements will be able to control supply so that producers' revenues can be raised above free market levels. For example, even though the International Rubber Organisation's (INRO) buffer stock was given additional financing in November 1985, the expansion of buffer stock capacity cannot go on indefinitely, both because of the financial burdens involved and because an ever-growing stockpile itself becomes a major negative influence on demand and prices. Thus, while INRO can hold up prices in the near term, after that the pressures of abundant supplies are likely to exert their influence on the market.

The buffer stock acquired under the International Tin Agreement (ITA) is, of course, already a major price depressant. With the collapse of the buffer stock in late October 1985, the ITA's support of the market ceased and effective prices fell. The prospective sale of the metal now owned by the buffer stock's creditors will prevent any major price increase for several years to come. Total world stocks are around 120,000 tonnes, versus non-communist world primary tin consumption of 150,000 tonnes per annum. Last year when ITA export controls were in effect, non-communist world

67

primary tin production was somewhat higher than consumption, and any output cutback from lower prices may well be offset by the lifting of export controls this year. Thus, even if the United States exercises restraint in sales from its Strategic Stockpile, tin prices and export revenues will be low for several years. In addition to the loss of export revenues, this will pose serious problems for Pacific Basin tin exporters like Malaysia, where much high-cost tin production will become uneconomic at free-market prices, forcing many small high-cost mines to close and thus creating unemployment. However, despite the Pacific Basin producers' strong incentives to seek to regain control of the tin market, an effective agreement is not likely. After all, a major reason why the buffer stock had to buy heavily to maintain prices within the range established by the ITA was the growth of output not subject to export controls. An agreement limited to the Pacific Basin producers would be even more vulnerable to outside competition.

In sharp contrast to tin, coffee is one commodity where an effective international commodity agreement continues to operate, partly because the US holds its hostility to the International Coffee Organisation (ICO) in abeyance due to its desire to stimulate the economies of the Latin American coffee producers. Indonesia, currently the world's third-largest producer after Brazil and Colombia, is likely to continue as a party to the ICO since the efficiency of the export control system is buttressed by the participation of many important consuming countries. Thus, in contrast to OPEC, a member country needs to keep within its quotas on its exports to major consumers, thus reducing the gains from cheating or withdrawing from the organisation. The Philippines is also a coffee producer and member of the ICO though its exportable production is only about one-ninth that of Indonesia.

Aside from coffee, other tropical beverages exported by the Pacific Basin countries such as tea and cocoa are not likely to be subject to effective commodity agreement control. On the positive side, this means that countries like Taiwan, Indonesia and Malaysia, on the one hand, will be free to expand export volumes without limitation and, as relatively minor suppliers, need not fear that their exports will have an important marginal effect on world prices.

Of the remaining agricultural commodities, including sugar, most of them are very heavily influenced by US and European agricultural policies, so that any commodity agreements could not provide Pacific Basin producers with an effective voice in market control such as that of the ICO. Nor are any market control agreements likely for the major commodities exported by Pacific Basin countries even where a few of them provide most of the world's supply. In the case of palm oil, for instance, Malaysia and Indonesia together produce over 70% of total world exports, but the availability of close substitutes such as soybean oil and coconut oil for many uses makes the probability of boosting prices above free-market level very low.

VIII Supply-side policies

So far, this chapter has focused mainly on the demand side of international commodity trade and on the possibility or lack thereof for exporters either in the Pacific Basin or outside of it to raise prices by controlling exports. It is important to point out the importance of factors affecting the supply of various commodities over the long term for the Pacific Basin producers and consumers.

The ability of the Pacific Basin exporters to retain or increase their role in world commodity markets will depend on whether scarce economic resources channelled into commodity production can, on average, earn as much for these producers as resources employed elsewhere, e.g. in manufacturing. This is particularly true for those Pacific Basin countries, such as Malaysia, Indonesia or the Philippines, that are major commodity producers but that have also attempted to develop an industrial potential over the past decade or so. The problem is further compounded by the competition that can exist between different products within the commodity sector, e.g. rubber versus palm oil in Malaysia, as well as between commodity production and other sectors, such as manufacturing and the production of rice for domestic consumption. In Australia, of course, long-run supply growth poses no problem given the country's highly developed economic base, free market philosophy and access to abundant capital, both foreign and domestic. New Zealand is also not likely to find it difficult to meet any growth in demand for its primary exports. However, in varying degrees, the other three commodity exporters—Malaysia, Indonesia and the

Philippines—could in some cases find it difficult to retain or expand their market share despite their urgent need to stimulate export revenues and support their rapidly growing populations. In recent years, the Indonesian commodity producing sector overall has made great progress, but continued future growth could be endangered by financial and non-economic constraints. Especially in light of the sharp drop in oil revenues, the government will not be able to fund investments to improve plantation and smallholder agriculture that would raise output and exports and create desperately-needed jobs. While the World Bank and other donors plan to provide about one-third of the necessary funds to upgrade Indonesia's agricultural production, a huge financing gap remains. In theory, private Indonesian and foreign capital could be used but the political and economic realities of Indonesian life make this very difficult. Even though some foreign companies operate rubber, tea, cocoa and palm oil plantations in Indonesia, any large-scale increase in foreign investment would most likely arouse strong political opposition, and existing regulation already contains strong disincentives for foreign firms, such as the relatively short terms for which leases can be obtained. While over time, political and institutional barriers are often eroded under the pressure of harsh economic reality, this is not inevitable. Thus, it is very possible that countries such as Indonesia will artificially limit their commodity exports in coming years by hindering opportunities for foreign investment in the commodity sector.

Chapter Four

ENERGY IN THE PACIFIC BASIN

I Introduction

The Pacific Basin group is a net energy importer even though it contains one OPEC member (Indonesia), and major exporters of other energy projects such as coal and liquified natural gas (LNG). However, Japan's immense weight as an energy consumer and the second-largest importer in the non-communist world is an important factor in the context of total energy consumption.

TABLE 4.1 PETROLEUM NET TRADE STATUS

Net exporters	Net importers
Indonesia	Australia
Malaysia	Hong Kong
	Japan
	New Zealand
	Philippines
	Singapore
	South Korea
	Taiwan

As shown in Table 4.1 looking at oil alone, only Indonesia and Malaysia are net exporters of petroleum, that is, exporting crude oil and refined petroleum products in excess of any imports of crude and refined products. All the other countries from Australia to Taiwan are net importers even though their import dependence (the share of net imports in total oil/energy needs) varies widely. They also differ widely in other aspects of their petroleum economy. Australia, for instance, by 1985 had become a significant exporter of crude oil even though oil import volumes exceeded crude exports, while Singapore remained a major international refining centre, importing large volumes of crude to process and re-export as refined products.

If we include all forms of commercial energy as shown below in Table 4.2, the picture changes slightly as Australia joins the ranks of net energy exporters.

TABLE 4.2   ALL COMMERCIAL ENERGY* NET TRADE STATUS

Net exporters	Net importers
Australia	Hong Kong
Indonesia	Japan
Malaysia	New Zealand
	Philippines
	Singapore
	South Korea
	Taiwan

Note: *Excluding traditional non-market funds

While the collapse of world oil prices since late 1985 could well have important effects on energy production and consumption, especially if prices stay depressed for several years, the current oil/ energy, import/export status in the Pacific Basin countries will probably not change greatly in the near term.

II   Japan

Oil is overwhelmingly Japan's most important energy source, providing nearly 4.5 mn bpd, about 60% of the total energy consumption. The second most important energy source is coal, which provides around 18% of the total, followed by natural gas (9%), and nuclear power (8%). The remaining 5% of Japan's primary energy nearly all comes from hydro-electricity, although there are small amounts of geothermal energy and various 'exotics' such as solar and wind power.

As Table 4.3 shows, oil's share of total primary energy consumption is much below 1973 levels due mainly to a more than five-fold increase in gas consumption and a more than twelve-fold growth in

TABLE 4.3   JAPAN: PRIMARY ENERGY SOURCES, 1973 VS. 1984

%

	1973	1984
Oil	75.8	59.4
Coal	16.9	18.4
Gas	1.6	9.2
Nuclear	0.7	8.0
Other	5.1	5.0
TOTAL:	100.0	100.0

nuclear power. While coal consumption also rose from 83 to 99 mn tons, coal provided less than one-fifth of the growth in non-oil energy supply, and hydro and other sources showed no growth over the period. This sharp decline in oil's relative importance due to growth in gas, nuclear power, and coal enabled Japan to cut its total oil consumption by nearly 14% over the period even though total energy consumption was up 7.5%. However, while energy consumption rose, due to conservation and other factors such as the declining importance of energy-intensive heavy industry, meant that growth in energy consumption lagged far behind economic growth. As a result, by the mid-1980s, the amount of energy Japan needed to produce every pound's worth of GNP was only 60% of the 1973 level.

As in various other areas of its economic life, Japan's shift away from oil and reduction in overall energy intensity reflected a combined public/private partnership to reduce national vulnerability to oil shocks of the type experienced in the 1970s. Along with a variety of other measures, such as encouragement to Japanese firms to undertake oil exploration and large-scale oil stock-piling, oil conservation and fuel-switching were intended to limit the political and economic costs associated with dependence on imported oil. Thus, with the major role of political/strategic concerns in shaping Japan's energy policies, low oil prices are not likely to be allowed to shift the country back to 1973 levels of oil dependence. In any event, prices for other fuel imports such as coal and LNG are at least partly sensitive to oil price declines, thus limiting purely economic incentives to shift back to oil. Nor are any 'post-Chernobyl' safety concerns likely to cause Japan to make any sharp cutbacks in reliance on nuclear power, so that the country's oil dependence will likely continue its gradual fall to about 55% by 1990 and 50% by the year 2000.

With domestic crude oil production only 10,000 bpd, Japan's oil has nearly all been imported, and until recently, most imports came in as crude oil. Refined product imports were tightly controlled, and nearly all took the form of naphtha and heavy fuel oil. Despite this protection, declining demand for petroleum products has forced the Japanese refiners to cut back capacity over the past few years. However, current capacity of 4.6 mn bpd is still well above that needed to meet domestic demand, especially as Tokyo is now opening up its markets to imports of gasoline and other light products under pressure from the US and other OECD nations. This will certainly mean further refinery shut-downs will occur over the next few years.

In line with its desire to diversify the sources of its oil and other energy imports, no single country supplies a major part of Japan's crude oil imports, the largest sources being the United Arab Emirates (21%), Saudi Arabia (17%) and Indonesia (11%). A significant fraction of non-oil energy supplies is also imported, including most of its coal and gas. Major sources of Japan's coal imports are Australia (68%), Canada (19%), USA (15%) and South Africa (9%). Major sources of gas, imported as LNG, are Indonesia, Brunei and Malaysia. In the future, Australia will be an important source. About three-quarters of Japan's LNG is used for electricity generation.

Japan continues to rely more heavily on oil for electric power generation than most other major western industrial countries, partly because environmental reasons favour burning significant quantities of very low sulphur crude oil and naphtha to produce electricity. However, in 1985 for the first time, nuclear power generation produced a larger proportion of electric power production (26%) than oil-fired power generation (25%). Gas-fired generation accounted for 21%, hydropower 16% and coal 10%. By 1986, Japan was already generating 10% of all nuclear electricity produced in the world, exceeded only by the USA (30%) and France (16%).

TABLE 4.4   NON-COMMUNIST WORLD AND SELECTED COUNTRIES NUCLEAR ELECTRIC POWER PRODUCTION, 1985

KwHr Bn

World total	**1,263.9**
USA	602.6
France	224.0
Japan	152.0
United Kingdom	59.6
South Korea	16.5
Taiwan	28.7

Given Japan's Hiroshima trauma, it is always conceivable that a nuclear accident, however minor and harmless to human health, could trigger a public outcry against nuclear power. Despite this, nuclear power is expected to supply 35% of Japan's electricity by the mid-1990s.

III   South Korea

Like Japan, South Korea has been seeking to reduce the petroleum share of energy consumption which is currently nearly 50%, down from 58% in 1981. Petroleum demand in 1984 was around 530,000 bpd, all imported, and typically oil comes in as crude and is refined domestically. Current refining capacity is 782,000 bpd.

Despite attempts at energy conservation and substitution of other fuels for oil, due to continuing rapid industrial growth, petroleum demand is expected to continue to grow over the next ten years, albeit less rapidly than total energy consumption. Coal is South Korea's only indigenous fossil fuel although domestic output supplies less than 60% of the country's consumption.

While oil continues to be the single most important energy source for South Korea's growing electric power system, coal and nuclear power also play a major role in the electricity system. In 1985, South Korea generated 16.5 bn Kilowatthours of nuclear electricity, nearly 18% of its total electric power production. There is also some hydro generation.

South Korea produces no natural gas, and in 1983 a 20-year contract was signed to import LNG from Indonesia. Assuming that disputes over pricing will be resolved, South Korea is scheduled to begin to receive LNG from the end of this year with shipments at a 2 mn ton annual rate. Like Japan, South Korea will use the LNG to generate electric power.

In addition to commercial fuels like oil, coal and nuclear, in South Korea as in many other developing nations, non-commercial fuels supply an important part of energy consumed in rural areas. With the replacement of traditional fuels like firewood by petroleum products, an intrinsic part of the development process, non-commercial fuels are likely to decline in importance in the future.

IV Taiwan

With its diplomatic isolation providing an added incentive to reduce dependence on imported oil, Taipei too has been seeking to reduce the petroleum share in its national energy balance. However, in 1986 petroleum, nearly all of it imported, supplied 58% of the country's primary energy requirements with oil consumption running at 300,000 bpd. Most products were refined domestically, with refining capacity currently at 543,000 bpd.

Aside from oil, other major sources of energy are coal (almost 18%), nuclear (nearly 17%), natural gas (4%) and hydroelectric power (3%). Imports also make up nearly four-fifths of the country's coal supplies, and with output declining, the import share will continue to rise. Domestic natural gas output is also declining, but Taiwan reportedly is negotiating for Indonesian LNG.

Under its programme to reduce dependence on imported oil, Taipei, like Seoul, has vigorously promoted nuclear power. Taiwan currently has three nuclear power stations operating and a fourth may be built. In 1985, Taiwan generated 28.7 bn Kilowatthours of nuclear electricity and nuclear power provided over 50% of the country's total electricity, a proportion surpassed by only France and Belgium.

Non-commercial fuels are of considerably less significance than in South Korea.

V Hong Kong

Hong Kong has no indigenous energy, and it imports petroleum and coal. Petroleum consumption is about 110,000 bpd, imported as refined products since the colony has no refinery. Fuel oil demand has fallen in recent years as the electric utilities have continued to switch to coal. There has been discussion of plans to import natural gas from China by pipeline and possibly nuclear-generated electricity.

VI Philippines

Underlying energy trends in the Philippines have been hard to discern as debt problems and political difficulties have depressed economic activity. In 1984, consumption of petroleum, the most important commercial primary energy source, was probably some 175,000 bpd, imported mainly in the form of crude oil. Refinery capacity is 216,000 bpd.

The 1984 oil demand levels reflected a sharp fall from previous years, due not only to general economic and political difficulties but also to substitution of coal, hydropower and geothermal energy for petroleum. This is in line with the national energy plan which targets to more than double the share of indigenous energy in the country's commercial energy supply.

The country's most important domestic energy potential is its geothermal energy resources. Indeed, even in 1982, geothermal and hydroelectric power supplied 13% of total commercial energy needs and some believe the Philippines could become the most important geothermal energy producer in the world.

The country's first nuclear plant, a 600 MW Westinghouse station, has been completed but has not yet been put into operation. The Aquino Government is concerned over safety, and there has also been controversy over cost and the role President Marcos played in decision-making related to the plant.

Non-commercial energy sources remain extremely important in the Philippines.

VII Singapore

With no indigenous sources, Singapore depends completely on oil imports to meet its energy needs. Domestic consumption is relatively small, about 100,000 bpd, with an additional 80,000 bpd used to bunker ships. Despite the relatively low levels of consumption the city-state plays an important role in world petroleum markets since it is a major export refining and petroleum trading centre while petroleum refining and petrochemicals have been significant elements in the national economy.

The basis for its major refining/trading role has been its refining capacity of 1mn bpd which has served to process imported crude oils and export refined products in many cases to Pacific Basin nations unable to meet their domestic needs for specific products such as diesel fuel from their own refineries. Frequently, refined products from Singapore are re-exported back to crude-supplying nations such as Indonesia, whose domestic refinery production does not match their internal consumption pattern.

Over the past year or two, it has seemed increasingly likely that Singapore's role as a refining centre will shrink even if its position in petroleum trading survives or is enhanced. The long-run decline in Singapore refining will result from the expansion of refining capacity in Indonesia, in the Mid-East OPEC countries, and in other countries such as India which have relied on imports from Singapore to balance out their product needs. For instance, Indonesia has recently completed investments in expanding/upgrading capacity in three refineries at Cilacap, Balikpapan and Dumai. While operations at these refineries initially have not been without difficulties, over the long term, this expansion in Indonesian capacity must largely eliminate its need to import products from Singapore.

Some industry analysts argue that Singapore's refining capacity should be cut in half, to only 500,000 bpd, but this could be unduly pessimistic. Recently, a number of processing deals, under which Singapore refiners run crude on a fee basis rather than buying crude and selling products, have helped the island's refining business, with China an important source of crude. Singapore has also processed oil from Iran, as well as Malaysia and Abu Dhabi and, intermittently, Indonesia.

In 1985, Singapore refineries ran an average 700,000 bpd of crude oil, and the figure for the first half of this year may be only slightly less. The opening-up of the Japanese product market and any boost to petroleum consumption from lower world oil prices will help the island's refining, and Malaysia reportedly is now in no hurry to proceed with the refineries it had planned. China's refinery-building plans will also affect Singapore's future and low oil prices could force Peking to cut back on refinery investments.

With regard to Singapore's purely domestic energy use, the government promotes conservation and is considering non-oil sources such as coal, solar power and natural gas. Despite agreement in principle, no formal contract is close on moving gas from Malaysia's offshore fields to Singapore for use in electric power generation, and declining Malaysian oil revenues have postponed plans to build a natural gas pipeline by at least a year. Previously, gas sales had been expected to begin in 1988.

VIII   Malaysia

With proven crude oil reserves of 3.1 bn barrels, Malaysia is now a significant crude oil exporter with crude oil output of 500,000 bpd, more than four times the level of a decade ago. Domestic consumption of this, at most 180,000 bpd, leaves a net export volume of over 300,000 bpd.

Malaysia has four refineries with a total capacity of 212,000 bpd. Besides oil, Malaysia is also an important player in natural gas markets. At 52.7 trillion cubic feet (TCF), the country's proven reserves are the largest in the Asia-Pacific area (Indonesia's gas reserves are 35.6 TCF) and Malaysia began LNG exports to Japan in 1983. In 1984, Malaysia accounted for 10% of world LNG exports, and exports to Japan are expected to rise substantially in the near term.

Besides providing export revenues, natural gas will also be an increasingly important source of energy for Malaysia's own domestic economy. Indeed, by the turn of the century, gas will have replaced oil as the nation's primary energy source. The government also hopes to increase and develop Malaysia's coal reserves and hydroelectric potential. In the early 1980s, hydropower provided about 3% of the country's commercial energy and imported coal less than 1%. Traditional fuels such as wood still account for the bulk of energy consumption in the rural sector of the economy.

IX Indonesia

Indonesia is an OPEC member and is the largest oil exporter in the Pacific Basin. Proven crude oil reserves are estimated at 8.5 bn barrels and crude oil output in 1985 averaged just over 1.256 mn bpd, significantly below the 1984 level and only 70% of capacity.

Although domestic consumption had been rising very rapidly since the early 1980s, several recent cutbacks in government subsidies to domestic prices have slowed down demand growth, and both relieved Jakarta's budgetary burdens and postponed the danger that rapid consumption growth would rapidly eliminate the country's exportable surplus of petroleum, its most important source of export revenue. Current domestic demand for petroleum is about 430,000 bpd and could expand slowly for a few years. However, over the long term as industrialisation spreads, consumption of oil to replace traditional non-commercial fuels which currently provide a huge share of rural energy needs must inevitably rise. Thus, besides ensuring levels of petroleum investment adequate to keep oil output from falling, the Jakarta regime must continue with efforts to conserve oil wherever this can be done without hampering economic growth.

Besides crude oil, the country is richly endowed with other energy resources such as natural gas, coal, hydro and geothermal power, and the regime is actively pursuing the development of such resources. The Suharto Government hopes that non-oil energy sources can cut domestic use of oil, thus making more oil potentially available for export, as well as generating export revenues in their own right. In developing both oil and non-oil energy resources, Indonesia has sought to attract foreign capital, and foreign investment is seen as essential to the functioning of the energy industry.

Indonesia's gas reserves of 35.6 TCF provide the basis for the largest LNG exporting industry in the world, accounting for 60% of the total and providing over half of Japan's LNG imports. LNG is currently Indonesia's second-largest export earner, in 1985 generating $3.8 bn to oil's $9 bn. However, the prospects for growth seem relatively limited even if successful arrangements can be made with South Korea and Taiwan since LNG is basically a regional commodity, not a world commodity like oil.

Excluding traditional fuels like wood, which are of major importance in rural areas, gas is the second most important energy source in Indonesia, in 1984 accounting for nearly 18% of total commercial energy, compared with 78% for oil. Gas consumption is currently held back by inadequate investment in transportation and distribution facilities, but a gradual increase is projected over the next few years. The government is also seeking to increase the use of coal, especially in electric power generation and in cement manufacturing, although currently it accounts for less than 1% of energy consumption. The country reportedly has 2.6 bn tons of recoverable coal reserves, but current output falls far short of current requirements for exports and domestic consumption. Jakarta has an ambitious programme designed to raise coal output from about 1 mn tonnes to around 12 mn tonnes by 1990. Hydro and geothermal power currently supply nearly 4% of Indonesia's energy needs. Currently there are 1,630 MW of hydropower, and there are plans to double this capacity. In addition, Indonesia has 10,000 MW of geothermal potential (250,000 bpd oil equivalent). Although much of this is likely to be uneconomic, there is one 30 MW and one 2 MW power station in operation, and several other projects are in various stages of development. Another 252 MW of geothermal capacity is planned.

Indonesia had hoped to have a nuclear power plant under construction by the end of the century to help meet the nation's chronic electricity shortage which will be exacerbated by economic growth and rising industrialisation. However, falling oil prices have greatly reduced Indonesia's financial resources and could also affect the economics of nuclear power versus other sources.

X   Australia

Australia is richly endowed with energy resources including coal, uranium and natural gas, as well as petroleum, Crude oil reserves total 1.5 bn barrels, and crude oil has been produced since 1964 though output remained relatively low until the 1970s. By early 1986, crude oil output had reached 565,000 bpd though output has since been cut back in response to the fall in oil prices. With domestic consumption of 600,000 bpd Australia is a net oil importer, although it exports about 20% of its crude and imports crude and products. The country also produces and exports some condensates (petroleum liquids found in natural gas) and naturally-occurring LPG. Current refining capacity is 622,000 bpd.

If oil prices remain well below 1985 levels, Australia will become decreasingly self-sufficient in petroleum due to falling output and continuing growth in demand, although consumption of petroleum products will grow more slowly than GNP and overall energy use. Thus, petroleum, which now accounts for 40% of Australia's energy, is expected to provide only 35% by the mid-1990s.

Coal is Australia's second most important energy source, with black coal providing 29% and brown coal a further 10%. Reserves total 34 bn tonnes for black coal and 47 bn tonnes for brown coal. At current rates, black coal output could be sustained for 200 years and brown coal output for even longer. More than two-thirds of Australia's output of black coal, 84 mn tonnes, is exported, and Australia is now the world's largest coal exporter. Despite exceptionally low production costs and the depreciation of the Australian dollar, some Australian producers are in financial difficulties due to the price cuts they were forced to accept during the recent world recession and, they claim, excessive taxation and freight charges. The industry also has industrial relations problems.

Natural gas is another of Australia's major energy resources with proven reserves of 18.2 bn cubic feet (about one-half Indonesia's proven reserves). Large-scale commercial use of natural gas began in 1969, and gas currently supplies 15% of domestic energy needs. Gas from the remote fields off northwest Australia will be exported to Japan in the form of LNG beginning in 1989 and peaking at 6 mn tonnes annually in 1993. This Northwest Shelf gas project is the largest investment project in Australian history.

Wood and bagasse (the residue from the crushing of sugar cane) together provide 5% of energy supplies and hydroelectric power about 1.5%. As nearly all of the economically attractive hydropower sites in Australia have been developed, little further growth can be expected from this source.

Even though the country has ample low-cost uranium reserves, Australia does not produce nuclear power since nuclear generation is not economic, especially as most of the Australian electricity authorities can build conventional power stations close to low cost coal reserves.

Solar energy currently supplies only a fraction of Australia's energy needs and is unlikely to be a significant energy source in the near future.

XI New Zealand

Hydro and geothermal power together are the single most important energy source providing 39% of the total as of 1984. Hydroelectricity accounted for 78% of total electricity and geothermal power another 5% with one large (160 MW) geothermal power station operating and another 100 MW plant to begin producing power in 1989.

In 1984, petroleum liquids (oil and condensate) were the second most important source of energy with total consumption of 76,000 bpd meeting 30% of domestic energy needs. With domestic liquids output (all condensates) of 18,000 bpd, most of the country's petroleum has had to be imported. Refining capacity was 53,000 bpd, well below consumption, so that much of the needed import volume has had to come in as products.

Coal supplied about 17% of energy needs in 1984 and gas 19%. Gas's importance began when the huge Maui gas field was discovered in 1969 and it grew dramatically when Maui started producing gas and condensate at the end of the 1970s. The New Zealand Government is pursuing a policy of substituting gas for oil, with heavy emphasis on replacing petroleum as an automotive fuel. In October, 1985, the New Zealand Synthetic Fuel Corporation started up a plant which converts natural gas to methanol and then to gasoline. At full capacity, this facility will produce 14,500 bpd of petrol, more than one-third of the country's current consumption. The plant uses Mobil Technology and is 75% owned by the government, 25% by Mobil. The plant cost US$ 1.2 bn, 20% below the sum originally budgeted.

The government is also trying to cut oil imports by promoting the conversion of vehicles to run on compressed natural gas and liquified petroleum gas.

Maui gas is also used to produce exported petrochemicals.

Chapter Five

BANKING AND CAPITAL MARKETS IN THE PACIFIC BASIN

I Introduction

The banking system plays a key role in the structure and development of an economy, and is an important tool of the government in carrying out its economic policies and development goals. This is certainly the case with the Pacific Basin countries where banking systems vary considerably from country to country but are central in understanding the structure of their economies, their level of economic development, and the means by which their governments carry out economic policy. This chapter will discuss the structure, size and scope of banking systems in the Pacific Basin along with financial market trends, the level of development of capital markets in the region, and the shift away from debt to other forms of financing. By way of definition, the banking system refers to the system of institutions which collect deposits, make loans, and serve as the primary vehicles for the government's economic and financial policies. The financial system refers to a broader range of organisations that play an intermediary role, but are secondary as they have more limited roles or scopes of activity. However, the lines between the primary banking system and secondary financial institutions are somewhat blurred. The banking system usually refers to commercial banks, and in some countries, other types of banks such as development or savings and loan banks. The broader financial system usually includes investment banks, pension funds, insurance and finance companies, mortgage firms, postal savings institutions, etc. As a country's financial system becomes more developed, for example in Japan, secondary financial institutions play a larger and more important role in the economy.

II Intermediation and savings

The banking system, and more broadly the financial system, are vital in intermediation, or channelling savings into investment. Direct government allocation and self finance are the two other ways of financing investment. The relative importance of these three methods of intermediation is determined by the structure of the economy, the level of economic development, and the policy goals of the government. In the Pacific Basin, the reliance on banking systems to intermediate is very important, and is growing as these countries look increasingly to the private sector to mobilise resources. In addition, for different reasons in each of the countries, most of the Pacific Basin governments are deregulating their banking systems in order to develop their financial markets further, strengthen their respective economies, and enhance their ability to deal with an increasingly difficult external environment. Most importantly, though, the development of banking systems in the Pacific Basin countries is allowing them to take better advantage of their high savings rates with resulting higher economic growth and investment. Table 5.1 shows that the savings rates in the Pacific Basin countries in 1983 either equalled, as with Australia, or exceeded, as with the rest of the countries, the average savings rates

TABLE 5.1   GROSS DOMESTIC SAVINGS RATES OF THE PACIFIC BASIN COUNTRIES (As % GDP)

World-wide industrial market economies	1965	1983
Japan	33	30
Australia	26	20
New Zealand	25	25
Average—All world-wide industrial market economies	23	20
World-wide upper middle-income economies		
Hong Kong	29	25
Singapore	10	42
South Korea	8	26
Malaysia	23	29
Average—All world-wide middle-income economies	24	23
World-wide lower middle-income economies		
Indonesia	6	20
Philippines	21	21
Average—All world-wide lower middle-income economies	16	17

Source: World Bank, 1985
Note: Taiwan is not a member of the World Bank so no data are available

of countries at comparable levels of development. A comparison of the countries' savings rates with comparable countries in 1965 shows that countries such as Singapore, South Korea, Malaysia and Indonesia have made substantial progress in increasing their savings rates.

III   Financial markets

The Pacific Basin financial markets, and specifically banking systems, can be broken down into three main groups, including the developed markets, the offshore financial markets, and the developing markets. The criteria for this breakdown include the depth and sophistication of the country's financial system as well as its scope and diversification. For example, Japan's financial system is one of the most sophisticated in the world, with a broad range of primary and secondary organisations playing diverse roles in financing economic activities. Hong Kong is an offshore financial centre where the majority of banking institutions are focused on international financial markets and activities rather than the domestic economy. Indonesia's financial system is characteristic of a developing market where there are only a few types of institutions, their services and expertise are somewhat limited, their scope is not broad, and they are not yet very flexible.

IV   The developed markets

Japan

Japan has the largest and most diverse financial market by far of all the Pacific Basin nations. In fact, five of its banks had over $100 bn in assets in 1985, with the largest US 'money centre' banks in size, scope of activities internationally, and level of sophistication. Twenty-five Japanese institutions are among the world's top 100 banks, and as shown in Table 5.2, 75 of them ranked among the world's top 500 in 1984. The banking system remains the primary source of capital and credit in Japan despite the development of diverse financial companies and bond and equity markets. Because of strict government regulation, however, there is as yet little integration between these diverse segments of the market, and the banks themselves are fairly specialised. One of the banking system's major roles over the past three decades has been to support the expansion of the industrial sector with an export orientation, and several of the largest banks are associated with the large industrial conglomerates that have played a major role in Japan's economic growth. In addition, under the supervision of the Central Bank, some of the largest banks at times play a semi-regulatory function in maintaining financial system liquidity.

TABLE 5.2 PACIFIC BASIN BANKS AND ASSETS AMONG WORLD'S TOP 500 BANKS 1984

Country	No. banks	Total assets (%) $bn	Total capital $bn	Capital assets (%)
Developed				
Australia	6	110.26	6.10	5.54
New Zealand	1	4.46	0.19	4.26
Japan	75	1,964.12	49.03	2.50
Basin centres				
Hong Kong	1	59.76	2.67	4.47
Singapore	4	17.87	2.21	12.36
Less developed				
Indonesia	3	14.77	0.77	5.24
South Korea	8	73.20	3.46	4.73
Malaysia	2	12.98	0.60	4.61
Philippines	2	9.63	0.58	6.03
Taiwan	8	41.56	1.43	3.43

Source: *The Banker,*

The Japanese banking system stands out from the others of the Pacific Basin not only on the basis of sheer size and level of sophistication. It also is characterised as having the lowest overall capital/asset ratios. This ratio is a measure of the capital strength of a bank or banking system. For example, in the United States, the regulatory agencies in the last few years have required higher levels of capital related to the size of the banks' assets in order to bolster their ability to withstand large losses from problem loans, such as in the areas of LDC debt, energy , or shipping. (When a loan goes bad, its loss is subtracted from the capital base of the bank; therefore, the larger the capital base, the stronger the ability of the bank to withstand loan losses.) The Japanese banks are considered to be undercapitalised if looking at published bank figures. However, the banks do have hidden, or unreported, reserves that may make their capital bases stronger than the capital asset ratio in Table 5.2 appears.

The 13 'city banks' are a major force in the banking system and traditionally account for about 60% of total banking system assets. Five from this group—Dai-Ichi Kangyo, Fuji, Sumitomo, Mitsubishi and Sanwa—are world-wide competitors with American giants like Citibank, and many of these 'city banks' are linked to the country's large industrial conglomerates. In addition to the city banks, there are over 60 regional banks that are similar to the city banks in the scope of their activities but focus their activities on medium and small enterprises outside of the large cities. Finally, there are numerous other types of banks, including 3 long-term credit banks, 7 trust banks, over 900 credit associations and co-operatives, 12 government-owned financial institutions, and about 4,120 farmers' co-operatives. This list does not include, however, several secondary financial institutions, including securities firms that act as investment banks, the Japan Development Bank, savings banks and postal savings institutions, insurance companies, pension funds, newly developed venture capital firms, and active stock and bond markets which have been growing rapidly in recent years.

Because of the specialisation in the banking system, different types of banks to some extent offer different types of services. For example, the regional banks primarily lend short term, the long-term credit banks lend primarily long term, while the trust banks straddle long and short term lending and are among the only banks to offer fiduciary services. However, the city banks dominate the country's financial markets, offering via 2,610 branches domestically and 241 branches abroad a wide range of services including industrial finance, consumer credit, leasing, foreign exchange operations and trust activities.

Australia

The Australian banking system is also highly developed, as it is both diversified and sophisticated. Three of its banks rank among the top 100 in the world with the largest—Westpac—having just over $30 bn in assets. In addition, six of its banks rank among the largest 500 in the world. There are several types of financial institutions in Australia, including savings, merchant and development banks, as well as secondary financial institutions such as mortgage companies, finance and insurance companies, pension funds and an active and growing stock market. In addition, as part of the overall climate of deregulation, foreign banks were allowed in 1985 to set up branches in Australia. Sixteen were licensed in that year, adding to over 80 foreign bank representative offices.

However, the primary banking system is dominated on a national level by the four largest commercial banks, called trading banks, and four government-owned banks. The four trading banks include Westpac, Australia and New Zealand Bank (ANZ), Commonwealth Banking Corp. and National Australia. They provide a variety of diversified short-term and long-term credit services, in addition to a broad spectrum of pension and investment services. Each of the four state-owned regional banks, the largest of which is State Bank of Victoria, has a regional focus and supports industrial concerns and other development priorities.

New Zealand

The New Zealand banking system, while small, is developed and sophisticated with strong ties to the Australian banking system. The country's largest trading bank, Bank of New Zealand, ranks as number 351 among the world's top 500 banks with assets of $4.4 bn. It is a government-owned bank and accounts for over 40% of all of the country's banking business. There are three other trading banks, however, including Westpac, the National Bank of New Zealand (a subsidiary of Lloyds) and ANZ. The four trading banks provide a variety of short-term credit services and are of particular importance in providing long-term financing for projects that fit in with the government's export goals. Other types of services, such as mortgages, leases, factoring and construction finance, are provided by merchant banks similar to Australian finance companies and formed by merger between foreign and domestic interests. Many New Zealand companies have looked abroad for their financing as domestic interest rates for long-term loans traditionally have been high, although the government development bank, the Development Finance Corporation, does lend to companies involved in areas of strategic economic interest.

V   Offshore financial centres

Hong Kong and Singapore are the Pacific Basin's most important offshore financial centres. Both Hong Kong and Singapore are essentially city-states with small domestic markets, and have deliberately developed and implemented regulatory frameworks to encourage free, open economic and financial systems. The Japanese Government's moves to deregulate its financial system are meant to turn Tokyo into an international financial centre, the Philippine Government has allowed the establishment of offshore banking units in Manila, there is some indication that the Chinese Government would like Shanghai to compete with Hong Kong as a financial centre, and there is a small offshore financial centre on the tiny Pacific island of Nauru. However, to date none of these can compete with either Hong Kong or Singapore.

An offshore financial centre technically is defined as a place where the banking system's activities and operations well exceed those needed by the domestic market. There are many factors that determine whether an offshore financial centre can survive, including the level and extent of reserve requirements, taxation, and exchange controls. In addition, liberal and flexible yet effective regulation, and environmental factors, such as the availability of trained staff, communications infrastructure, and time zone location, are also important. Examples of offshore financial centres, in addition to Hong Kong and Singapore, are the Bahamas, Bahrain and Panama. However, if New York and London are included (they certainly meet many of the criteria of an offshore financial centre), the line between offshore and onshore becomes somewhat blurred. Offshore financial centres play a major role in the Eurocurrency market world-wide (defined as the sum of lending in foreign currencies to both residents and non-residents of the country in which the lending bank is located). Table 5.3 gives a breakdown of the Eurocurrency market world-wide and the importance of Hong Kong and Singapore in it.

TABLE 5.3   EXTERNAL EUROCURRENCY CLAIMS BY BANKING COUNTRY 1975–1874

$ bn, year-end

	1975	1980	1984	% growth 1975–1984	Share in total 1984
Europe, N. America, Japan					
UK	118	334	463	292.4	29.1
Japan	19	49	87	357.9	5.5
Canada	13	35	40	207.7	2.5
USA	2	4	11	450.0	0.7
Other Europe	140	417	458	227.1	28.8
Sub-Total	292	839	1,059	262.7	66.6
Offshore financial centres					
Cayman Islands	0	85	131	54.1*	8.2
Bahamas	55	125	125	327.3	7.9
Singapore	13	45	101	676.9	6.4
Hong Kong	9	38	77	755.6	4.8
Bahrain	2	31	53	255.0	3.3
Panama	8	34	32	300.0	2.0
N. Antilles	0	7	12	71.4*	0.8
Sub-Total	87	365	531	510.3	32.7
TOTAL	379	1,204	1,590	773.0	100.00

Source: Bank for International Settlements, 1985.
Note:*   Average from 1980

Hong Kong

Hong Kong has a very sophisticated banking system and is the third largest offshore financial centre in the world in terms of volume of banking transactions and investment management. In addition, the financial system is becoming more sophisticated in the types of financial instruments available, and the stock market also has developed in depth. The banking system is comprised of three tiers of institutions which are differentiated by the types of deposits which they can accept. The most important of these are the 141 commercial banks—35 are domestic and 106 are foreign—which are allowed to accept all deposits and conduct traditional banking business.

Only one of these banks, Hong Kong and Shanghai Bank, ranks among the world's 500 largest, yet with almost $60 bn in assets, it ranked 28th in the world in 1985. In fact, this bank plays a special role in Hong Kong which lacks a central bank. Hong Kong and Shanghai Bank is one of two note-issuing institutions in the territory, and the government uses this bank, among a few other domestic banks, to exert some regulatory control when necessary.

In addition, there are two types of deposit taking companies, called DTCs. The 283 registered DTCs may accept deposits larger than HK$ 50,000 with a maturity of at least three months, while the 34 licensed DTCs can only accept deposits larger than HK$ 500,000. The latter DTCs act as investment banks while the former act as savings and mortgage institutions. Finally, the Hong Kong market includes about 280 insurance companies.

Singapore

Singapore's Government established the offshore market in 1968 through deliberate policy, and set up the Monetary Authority of Singapore (MAS) in 1972 to regulate the market and carry out the functions of a central bank. Since then, Singapore's financial system has grown in depth and complexity to compete with Hong Kong. There is a wide variety of institutions and sub-markets competing with each other, but the 130 commercial banks are the most important source of capital in Singapore. Four of these banks— Development Bank of Singapore, United Overseas Bank, Overseas Chinese Bank and Overseas Union Bank—rank among the world's top 500 banks and dominate the domestic market. There are, as well, just over 100 foreign commercial banks represented in Singapore. In addition to the commercial banks, there are 4 discount houses, 34 finance companies, 55 merchant banks, 54 representative offices, 8 international money brokers and 174 Asian Currency Units (ACUs). The latter are commercial banks and merchant banks that participate in the Asian Currency Market. That in turn is comprised mostly of the Asian Dollar Market (ADM), and Singapore's is the largest in the Pacific Basin, overtaking Hong

Kong and Tokyo in size of assets. The ADM competes with the local money market, the foreign exchange market, and the new Singapore International Money Exchange (SIMEX).

In early 1987 the Government plans to introduce a new market for government bonds. This will be followed by markets in corporate bonds, negotiable CDs and other tradeable securities.

VI   The developing markets

The developing country banking systems in the Pacific Basin include those of Indonesia, South Korea, Malaysia, the Philippines and Taiwan. They are characterised, in general, by the dominance of banks over other types of financial institutions, the high degree of government ownership or control of financial assets, the key development role played by the banks under government direction or influence, and lack of depth and sophistication in the financial system as a whole. Table 5.4 demonstrates for Indonesia, South

TABLE 5.4   FINANCIAL MARKET COMPOSITION IN SELECTED PACIFIC BASIN DEVELOPING COUNTRIES

As % of total financial assets	Indonesia	South Korea	Philippines
Capital market			
Non-securities market			
Central bank	D	S	M
Commercial banks	D	D	D
Development/specialised banks	S	D	M
Non-bank financial institutions	S	S	S
Securities market	S	S	S
Money market	S	S	S
Informal market	S	M	M

Source: Asian Development Bank, 1986

Notes: D=Dominant (controls more than 40% of total financial assets)

M=Moderate (controls 10–39%)

S=Small (controls less than 10%)

Korea and the Philippines the key role played by the commercial banks in the financial system. In all three countries, non-bank financial institutions, the securities market and the money market are not really significant, illustrating the lack of depth. The informal market, or that segment of the financial system outside of government control and regulation (i.e. the 'kerb' market in South Korea) is not insubstantial in either South Korea or the Philippines, reflecting that the formal market does not fully meet the financial needs of the economy. In addition, the extent of government control of financial assets, which is not reflected in these figures, is estimated at between 40% and 70%, certainly indicating the pre-dominance of government in the financial sector.

Indonesia

There are four types of commercial banks in Indonesia, including government-owned banks, private banks, regional development banks, and foreign-owned bank branches. However, the banking system is dominated by 5 large state-owned commercial banks that provide the broadest range of services and account for more than 80% of the country's financial assets. Three of these banks—Bank Negara Indonesia, Bank Bumi Daya and Bank Dagang Negara—are among the 500 largest banks in the world, although none ranks among the top 100. These five banks play a major role in supporting the government's development goals. In fact, each of these banks is assigned responsibility for a priority sector and receives subsidised central bank funding and public sector company deposits in order to carry out financial activities in line with the government's priorities. Thus, it is these banks that played important roles in funding the development of Indonesia's commodity, and in particular, oil sectors, and now are involved in financing the country's agro-industrial enterprises. In addition, however, there are 26 regional banks, 10 foreign banks and 75 private banks which compete with a variety of other financial institutions, such as investment finance corporations, insurance and leasing companies, and credit co-operatives. However, all but the state-owned commercial banks are limited in scope and generally local in service provision.

South Korea

The most important sources of capital in the South Korean banking system are deposit taking institutions that include 65 commercial banks and 3 specialised banks. Together they accounted for over 55% of all loans in 1984. Of the commercial banks, the seven nation-wide city banks provide over 40% of all won loans and 20% of all foreign currency loans in the country. Five of the seven—Bank of Seoul, Korea First, Commercial Bank of Korea, Hanil Bank and Cho-Heung Bank—are among the largest 500 banks in the world. In addition, one of the three specialised banks, Korea Exchange Bank, is not only among the top 500 but is also the largest in South Korea. Other commercial banks include 10 provincial banks and 52 foreign bank branches. Finally, there are several development banks in South Korea, and two of them—Korea Development Bank and Small and Medium Industry Bank—are among the 500 largest in the world. There are numerous savings banks, insurance companies, short-term finance firms and merchant banks but they are far less important than the commercial banks, specialised banks and development banks.

The banking system as a whole is tightly controlled by the government, despite its moves to deregulate the system. It is not only an important tool in the limiting of inflationary pressures, a priority for this export-driven economy, but also is a means for supporting government policy towards the industrial sector. For two decades, government policy encouraged bank lending to the large industrial conglomerates. However, that policy shifted in 1985 as the government encouraged credit extension to small and medium sized firms that were more flexible and able to take advantage of changes in the external environment.

Malaysia

Thirty-eight commercial banks dominate the financial sector in Malaysia, and the most important of them are either partially or totally government owned. The two largest—Bank Bumiputra and Malayan Banking Berhad—rank among the largest 500 in the world. Bank Bumiputra is 100% government owned, and the largest private bank is only fourth-largest in the country. In 1984, the state-owned oil company acquired 90% of Bank Bumiputra's stock under special legislation, taking over all of the bank's $1 bn debt. The latter had been incurred in large part as a result of the near-failure of the bank's Hong Kong subsidiary when it invested in numerous real state loans to Chinese developers. With the collapse of the Hong Kong real estate market in the early 1980s, these developers failed as well. The resulting scandal has embarrassed the Malaysian Government, whose official development policies favour the advancement of the indigenous Malay majority ('bumiputra') over the wealthy Chinese minority. In fact, the banks are required to extend at least 20% of their loans to entities owned by or favouring the 'bumiputra' populace, and there are required levels of housing loans to bumiputras, as well.

In addition to the commercial banks, there are 12 merchant banks that offer a wide variety of investment services and can accept deposits from other financial institutions. All merchant banks are Malaysian majority owned joint ventures between foreign and Malaysian interests, and their influence in the country's financial system has been growing rapidly in recent years. A second tier of financial institutions, including savings banks, insurance companies and finance companies, fairly well developed. Finally, several development banks, the most important of which is Malaysian Industrial Development Finance BhD, foster development of a variety of industrial ventures with a focus on those owned or benefiting the bumiputra populace.

Philippines

The Philippine financial system is relatively well developed, although it has suffered in recent years from the country's economic and political crisis. The commercial banks are dominant in the sector and offer primarily short-term credit, although other financial institutions such as finance companies, insurance companies and investment houses may offer similar services. Government institutions have been the traditional source of medium- and long-term credit, although the long-term capital market as well as the stock market have diminished in scope and activity as a result of the country's recent problems. This, however, appeared to begin changing with the fall of the Marcos Government and the advent of the Aquino Government and greater confidence in the economy generally.

There are 34 commercial banks in the Philippines, and 28 are privately owned 2 are government owned, and 4 are foreign owned bank branches. The Philippine National Bank, the largest commercial bank, and the Development Bank of the Philippines (DBP) are both government owned and rank among the world's top 500 banks. The DBP offers medium- and long-term credit in sectors and areas identified as priorities for economic development by the government, and receives substantial funding from both the government and multinational and bilateral official sources. In 1976, the central bank implemented regulations allowing foreign banks to form offshore banking units (OBUs) that take deposits and provide loans in foreign currency. While the Manila OBU market in a way challenges Hong Kong or Singapore, 26 foreign banks now operate OBUs in Manila, while 22 local banks and 2 foreign banks are licensed under the foreign currency deposit unit system (FCDU). Other financial institutions in the Philippines include investment banks, savings banks, insurance companies, and other government sources of long-term credit (such as the social security system).

Taiwan

The Taiwanese financial system is predominantly government owned, and is generally considered to be less developed than other sectors in the economy. The high level of government ownership has impeded its flexibility and has contributed to the large size of the informal 'kerb' market. The collapse of several financial entities of the Cathay Group in early 1985 sent shock waves through the Taiwanese economy and exposed the vulnerability of the financial system due to reliance on 'kerb' market and lax oversight by financial officials. Recent government measures are aimed not only at reducing government control as a means of increasing banking system flexibility, but also at tightening regulatory supervision and accounting standards in order to prevent further scandals. This is particularly important in maintaining confidence, an issue for political reasons with which the government is very concerned. Moreover, the strength of the banking system is the key as it is the government's main tool in controlling inflationary pressures emanating from excess export revenues.

The financial system is comprised of 24 local commercial banks, 31 foreign bank branches, 75 credit co-operatives, 282 farmers' co-operatives, 23 insurance companies, a postal credit system, and several other types of credit organisations. Eight of the country's local commercial banks are among the world's 500 largest. High-lighting the extent of government ownership, only one of the eight is privately owned. The commercial banks, whether government or privately owned, provide predominantly short-term credit (as well as other services) and almost all lending is collateral-based, reflecting the inadequacy of accounting standards and credit analysis. The government banks do provide some investment banking services although eight trust banks have been formed to provide a broader range of investment activities. The lending of government-owned commercial banks, however, is focused on providing short-term capital to priority sectors, and in particular, for high technology development. There are several development banks, the most important of which is the China Development Corp., a majority privately held institution with some foreign ownership. It is one of the few sources of long-term capital. The other, the government-owned Bank of Communications, is involved in medium- and long-term financing in heavy and strategic industries.

VII   Financial trends in the Pacific Basin

There are numerous changes affecting banking and finance in the Pacific Basin which mirror broader world-wide trends. They include financial deregulation, banks' increasing involvement in equity market activities, and a general shift by the governments from borrowing on syndicated loan markets to tapping their own credit markets and international bond markets. These result in part from policies of the US Government and multilateral organisations emphasising the role of the private sector within the context of free markets, as well as the general realisation by governments and banks that the build-up of bank debt has become increasingly problematic. Finally, governments have decided that commercial banks are not capable alone of financing economic development. The backdrop for all of this are the current period of disinflation in most countries that has increased the burden of debt held by banks in stagnant sectors such as real estate, energy, shipping and commodities; the shift from bank deposits to money market deposits that offered higher (unregulated) interest rates; the consequent deregulation of commercial bank deposit rates; the 'securitisation' of debt as banks become involved in capital market and securities activities; and the reduction of commercial bank lending to developing countries.

All of these world-wide trends have to varying degrees begun to change the nature of banking in the Pacific Basin. Deregulation is having the most impact in the region, particularly as governments promote private sector development, strengthen the banking systems' ability to finance economic growth, and rely increasingly on domestic markets to finance development. In many Pacific Basin countries, the banking systems are suffering from a mismatching of assets and liabilities: i.e. the banks make medium- and long-term loans, but are unable to attract medium- or long-term deposits. The implicit deregulation—of interest rates and types of instruments which the banks may offer—to correct this is necessary but may run counter to other economic priorities, thus creating a real dilemma for many of the region's governments. However, it is a challenge that must be addressed if broader economic development goals are to be achieved.

Japan has probably gone furthest down the path of deregulation, for both domestic and external reasons. Domestically, the development of bond markets outside of the control of the government necessitated deregulation, while the US Government pressured the Japanese to boost the value of the yen by opening the financial market to foreign investors. Measures to deregulate were first introduced in the late 1970s, although their pace and scope made greatest headway in 1985. For example, the banks are being allowed to expand their equity market activities and to trade government bonds, while deposit interest rate liberalisation and a government futures bond market were commenced. In addition, the Ministry of Finance has recently proposed a new capital/assets ratio standard of 5% in order to strengthen the financial system. As a result of these and other measures, there is increased competition in the Japanese market, although the overall level of restrictions still is substantial, and thus modifies the pace of deregulation. Australia and New Zealand are also moving towards more market-orientated economic policies, and as a result, are implementing deregulating measures in the financial sector. Australia, in particular, has moved along these lines, and in 1983, opened its market to foreign banks while encouraging its banks to enter foreign markets.

In Hong Kong and Singapore, regulatory trends in recent years have focused more on strengthening control over the financial system without hampering overall international competitiveness.

This is particularly the case in Hong Kong where several bank failures and problems with Ka Wah and Union Banks have revealed the lack of supervision over the financial system. Since 1984, changes to the Banking Ordinance have increased bank supervision and balance sheet disclosure requirements, and raised capital adequacy ratios. In Singapore, where banking system supervision was generally tighter than in Hong Kong, the economic downturn has had a deleterious effect on the banks. In 1984 and 1985, changes to the Banking Act have strengthened the MAS' (Monetary Authority of Singapore) already stringent control and broadened its scope in overseeing insurance and securities activities.

In the developing countries of the Pacific Basin, deregulation is proceeding, albeit at a slower pace. It is viewed in most of the countries as necessary to support the move towards more open, freer markets, to stimulate the private sector, to increase economic flexibility and to deepen financial markets. However, it is a slow process, and some of the countries are having more success than others. Taiwan and South Korea have perhaps done most to deregulate their financial systems, although South Korea has been more effective at it than Taiwan.

In Korea, liberalisation began in 1980. In 1982 and 1983, the government banks were privatised, new market instruments were introduced, and interest rate deregulation was begun in order to attract 'kerb' market funds into the banking system. In 1984, a three-year plan was introduced to permit both foreign and domestic banks to operate along similar lines, with the intention of increasing competition within the market. This has been accompanied by policies focusing on the development of small and medium sized industries with an emphasis on technological development and increasing the flexibility of the economy overall. In Taiwan, the government is attempting to relax government controls in order to increase the banking system's responsiveness to the private sector. In 1985, controls were relaxed on foreign banks, a new interbank system (SWIFT) linking Taiwan to international financial markets was to be tested for implementation, the stock market was opened, and some interest rate liberalisation was begun. However, the process in Taiwan is proceeding slowly.

In the other developing countries of the Pacific Basin, there has

TABLE 5.5   FOREIGN DEBT OF THE PACIFIC BASIN NATIONS

	Japan	Australia	New Zealand	Hong Kong	Singapore	Indonesia	South Korea	Malaysia	Philippines	Taiwan
Total debt (US$ bn)										
1983	119.1	32.1	10.3	7.9	2.0	29.5	40.1	15.0	26.4	10.0
1985	148.0	51.1	14.6	9.5	3.7	37.0	48.0	20.3	26.3	7.8
Debt/GDP (%)										
1983	10.3	20.5	43.7	27.8	13.4	37.3	53.5	53.1	77.2	20.1
1985	11.2	33.0	65.5	27.8	21.8	45.5	57.7	63.1	86.6	13.0
Short-term debt (US$ bn)										
1983	70.3	10.0	1.7	3.3	0.2	5.9	16.7	2.7	12.3	3.5
1985	34.0	17.0	2.6	3.7	0.3	8.7	16.8	4.2	9.7	3.4
Short-term debt/total debt (%)										
1983	59.3	31.1	16.9	41.1	12.0	20.1	41.6	17.8	46.5	35.5
1985	23.0	33.3	17.5	39.2	8.1	23.5	35.0	20.7	37.1	42.9
Commercial bank debt/total (%)										
1983	n/a*	58.1	43.2	n/a*	n/a*	44.9	57.9	66.6	59.8	62.5
1985	n/a*	51.0	44.0	n/a*	n/a*	40.5	69.8	63.1	55.1	67.9
Debt service ratio (%)										
1983	8.3	26.5	22.2	9.5	6.3	15.1	18.7	9.8	35.6	7.2
1985	9.7	33.2	23.6	6.4	6.1	24.5	19.7	12.2	38.5	6.7

Source: Morgan Guaranty, 1984, 1986
Note: *Data not available for countries where banks are major international financial intermediaries

been less progress to date on financial deregulation. It is true that the Philippines has a relatively advanced banking system that provides a wide range of financial services. However, the economic and political crisis of recent years has limited the resources of financial institutions, and by 1984, lending had almost stopped because of the high rate of bankruptcies. However, with the advent of the Aquino Government, this may all change, although it is still too early to predict how long it will take for both the economy and the banking system to recover. Malaysia's financial sector is also relatively developed, although the government is still predominant. In recent years, it has focused on developing the private sector along with advancing the 'bumiputra' population. However, there has been little effort to deregulate *per se*; rather, the government has been concerned with banking system liquidity since the slump in commodity revenues and economic growth began in 1984. There has been some relaxation of foreign equity rules to stimulate investment, but not in the financial sector. Finally, Indonesia's banking system is the least developed of the Pacific Basin countries, although it has received official donor aid in recent years to hire consultants and train personnel to increase the capabilities of the financial sector. However, while the government liberalised some banking system regulations in 1982 and 1983, the dominance of the government-owned banks and the strong regulatory environment continue to limit the impact of free market forces.

Deregulation, as noted above, has accompanied the efforts by Pacific Basin governments to develop their own capital markets as an alternative to borrowing from commercial banks both domestically and abroad. Chapters One and Two discussed the foreign indebtedness of the Pacific Basin countries. By way of brief review, additional foreign debt statistics are found in Table 5.6. Japan, Hong Kong and Singapore, as the region's financial intermediaries, are not borrowers, and in fact the banks in those countries and Taiwan are capital exporters. Indeed, according to Bank for International Settlements (BIS) data, Japanese banks accounted for almost all new international bank lending in 1984, rising by 63%. Meanwhile, US bank lending abroad fell by 16.5% and UK bank lending by 9.5%. The major Pacific Basin borrowers are the five developing countries of the region. While Australia and New Zealand have fairly substantial foreign debts, especially as compared to the size of their economies, the flexibility of their economies and access to international capital markets mitigates the risks associated with their debt.

The foreign debt of the developing countries of the region is of most concern. The Philippines has the highest debt/GDP ratio of all the countries in the region, indicating the highest burden relative to the economy, and it has had an IMF standby agreement that includes a loan of $603 mn and an IMF-approved economic austerity programme since 1984. In addition, the government negotiated a rescheduling agreement with its foreign bank creditors in 1984 which included a new loan of $900 mn, and rescheduled official debt within the Paris Club. Both the bank and IMF loans were suspended in early 1986 because the failing Marcos Government had not maintained its commitments under the IMF-approved economic programme. The Aquino Government is negotiating with the IMF to extend the expiration of the IMF standby so that it can meet its economic targets and receive the remainder of both the IMF and bank loans.

Korea's foreign debt is also quite large, although the government has had no problems in servicing the debt or maintaining the confidence of its foreign bank creditors. This is largely due to the perceived ability of the Korean Government to manage competently its foreign debt as well as the country's economy. However, foreign bank creditors continue to watch Korea carefully, particularly its

TABLE 5.6 EXTERNAL DEBT BY REGION

	Asia		Western Hemisphere		Africa		Middle East		Europe	
	1980	1984	1980	1984	1980	1984	1980	1984	1980	1984
External debt (US$ bn)	14.6	179.3	192.6	310.5	50.9	70.7	36.3	56.2	67.2	76.6
Debt/exports (%)	67.5	79.9	187.0	273.3	143.2	215.8	110.7	161.8	117.7	121.0
Debt/GDP (%)	15.9	21.3	27.3	57.6	35.7	61.8	51.7	49.2	25.0	37.6
Debt service ratio (%)	8.4	10.5	34.1	42.7	17.4	24.3	12.1	21.9	19.8	21.6

Source: World Bank, 1985

export performance and the potential for political upheaval that might affect creditor confidence in 1986. Both Malaysia and Indonesia have borrowed substantially from foreign banks, particularly as their export proceeds from commodity and oil exports have slumped. However, they continue to borrow freely and the rates charged to them have fallen as the overall number of credit-worthy developing country borrowers has declined.

Table 5.6 illustrates the relatively low level of foreign debt in Asia as compared to the other regions of the world. Despite this, the Pacific Basin countries are shifting towards greater reliance on bond and equity financing and away from commercial bank syndicated loan borrowing as part of the broader trends discussed above. Table 5.7 shows the rapid growth in bond and CD (certificate of deposit) financing in the Pacific Basin capital market between 1984 and 1985, while the expansion of syndicated bank loans was much more moderate. The bond markets in the Pacific Basin countries are dominated by their governments, which are the primary issuers of bonds. Banks are required to purchase and trade a specific amount of bonds, and secondary markets have arisen as a result of those requirements rather than risk or rate considerations.

TABLE 5.7 GROWTH IN PACIFIC BASIN CAPITAL MARKET ACTIVITY: TOTAL BUSINESS RECORDED

US$ mn	1984	1985	Increase (% change)
Bonds	19,400	51,200	164
CDs	2,400	4,126	72
Sydicated loans and notes	17,700	21,232	20
TOTAL	39,500	76,562	94

Source: *Asia Banking*, 1986

Gross direct investment, portfolio investment and stock market development have increased partly as a result of the shift away from bank financing towards investment and equity financing. Table 5.8 demonstrates the expansion of direct investment and portfolio investment in the region. Stock markets have also grown in size; Japan's market is the largest and most highly developed, and the total value of stock traded is in the order of $225 bn as compared to New York's valued at $1,500 bn. The markets of Hong Kong, Singapore and Malaysia are the largest in the region excluding Japan with their markets valued at over $25 bn and comparing to the larger European markets. The stock markets in Taiwan and South Korea are in the $5–$15 bn range and compare to the smaller European markets. The stock markets in Indonesia and the Philippines are the smallest in the region, are valued at under $3 bn, and are not very significant. The listings in most of the developing countries of the region are concentrated in a few major sectors, such as industrial organisations in South Korea, oil and mining in the Philippines, and major joint ventures in Indonesia. The level of participation is still low, and secondary markets are characterised as weak, leading to the conclusion that there is a lot of untapped potential in these markets provided that the regulatory framework and broader economic and political environment support their development.

TABLE 5.8   INTERNATIONAL EQUITY INVESTMENT

SDRs mn						
	1979	**1980**	**1981**	**1982**	**1983**	**1984**
Gross direct investment	26,464	36,668	49,399	44,370	43,650	51,356
Industrial nations	22,607	27,608	31,579	22,582	27,240	36,342
All developing nations	3,856	9,060	17,820	21,787	16,410	15,014
Asia	1,806	2,737	4,097	4,225	4,485	4,152
Asia's share of developing nations total (%)	46.8	30.2	23.0	19.4	27.3	27.6
Portfolio investment	−2,327	−13,393	−23,005	−17,304	−2,305	22,073
Industrial nations	−1,804	3,465	2,036	−9,370	−8,928	6,710
All developing nations	−523	−17,758	−25,041	−7,933	6,623	15,363
Asia	365	160	1,153	2,128	1,327	1,400

Source: IMF, 1985

Chapter Six

SOCIAL ISSUES IN THE PACIFIC BASIN

The Pacific Basin contains Asia's most prosperous countries: Japan, Taiwan, South Korea, Malaysia, Singapore, Australia and New Zealand. Although some of the problems typical of developing countries exist in Indonesia and the Philippines, i.e. malnutrition, illiteracy, substandard housing, inadequate medical care and poverty, on the whole the social problems of the region tend to be more complex. Religious and ethnic tension, youth and labour unrest, and other problems associated with rapid change and unaccustomed prosperity prevail, particularly in family and family-planning issues. Overall, the question is whether social policies such as those implemented in Japan and Malaysia which have sought to graft modern technology and economic concerns onto a traditional cultural infrastructure can create a stable social order.

I Religious and ethnic tensions

Religious and ethnic tension is unusual in the largely homogenous countries of the Pacific Basin, except in Malaysia and Indonesia where Islamic fundamentalism has become tied in with political and economic issues.

In Malaysia, Islam has become identified with the Malay nationalist cause. Following Malay-Chinese race riots in 1969, Dr Mahathir Mohamed, now the country's prime minister, wrote a famous position paper entitled 'The Malay Dilemma', which was then incorporated into the foundation of the government's political and economic strategy, the New Economic Policy. Mahathir concluded that the economic gap between the poor Malays and the rich Chinese had to be narrowed in order to avoid repetition of the trouble. He introduced a number of measures giving indigenous Malays, or 'bumiputras', a greater share in the country's riches as well as in the language of instruction although Malay speakers are a bare majority in the population. Islam, which is synonymous with being a Malay, was given religious supremacy as well.

However, Mahathir's programmes were and remain essentially conservative and have not moved fast enough to satisfy Islamic leaders who want their mullahs to have power over secular policies, such as democratisation of access to education, fighting corruption, and better political access for neglected areas. An Islamic bank, Islamic insurance and Islamic university courses have been announced.

Mahathir's allegiance to Islam has created serious problems for him particularly in the state of Sabah where fundamentalist leaders have initiated bombings and riots in order to gain federal control. There are thought to be 300,000 Filipinos in Sabah, most of them Muslims from the southern Philippines. Many are poor and unemployed, and have proved a fertile recruiting-bed for the insurgents, who have paid them $10–$20 a day to protest.

Sabah shares the Subic Sea with the Philippines' historically troublesome island of Mindanao, and has harboured Filipino separatists, including members of the Moro Liberation Front, for years. The current government of Sabah, which is controlled by the predominantly Christian Kadozans, feels that previous (Muslim) state governments have encouraged illegal Filipino immigration to increase the size of the state's Muslim population. Moves are underway to deport many jobless militant Muslims back to the Philippines just as President Aquino is trying to stabilise her country's restless Islamic south. This may seriously strain relations between Malaysia and the Philippines.

II Population and family issues

The Pacific Basin contains some of Asia's most populous countries (See Table 6.1). A variety of family planning programmes has been a key policy factor in nearly all of the developing countries of the region, for it is commonly felt that many social and economic problems have their roots in the demographic situation. However, some curious trends are surfacing.

In Singapore and other societies where the population base is primarily Chinese, doctors remain unable to convince educated working women that a healthy baby, rather than a healthy male baby, is the goal of pregnancy. There is no rural sector in Singapore,

TABLE 6.1 KEY VITAL STATISTICS IN ASIA AND OCEANIA

Country	Est. mid-1983 pop (mn)	Average annual birth rate (per 1000) 1975–80	Average annual death rate (per 1000) 1975–80	Infant mortality rate (per 1000 live births) 1975–80	Annual population increase (%) 1975–80	Doubling rate (years)	Life expectancy at birth (years) 1975–80 males	females	GNP per head (US$) 1983
Asia:									
Afghanistan	17.2†	48.9	27.0	205	0.79	88.1	36.6	37.3	n/a
Bangladesh	94.7	47.2	18.9	140	2.83	24.8	47.1	46.1	130
Bhutan	1.4	40.0	19.8	156	2.02	34.7	44.6	43.1	n/a
Burma	36.7	38.5	14.2	107	2.43	28.9	51.0	54.1	180
China (inc. Taiwan)	1,039.7	22.0	7.6	49	1.44	48.5	62.6	66.5	290*
Hong Kong	5.3	18.6	4.4	13	2.73	25.7	68.8	75.5	6,000
India	732.3	36.1	14.6	129	2.15	32.6	51.2	50.0	260
Indonesia (excl. E. Timor)	156.4‡	36.4	15.1	99	2.14	32.7	48.7	51.3	560
Korea (Dem. People's Rep.)	19.2	32.5	8.3	37	2.42	29.0	60.5	64.6	n/a
Korea, Repub.	40.0	25.3	8.1	34	1.55	45.1	62.4	68.8	2,010
Laos	4.2	43.1	17.3	135	2.59	27.1	46.1	49.0	n/a
Malaysia	14.9‡	30.8	6.9	33	2.39	29.3	63.5	67.1	1,870
Mongolia	1.8	37.1	8.3	59	2.82	24.9	60.5	64.6	n/a
Nepal	15.7	44.6	20.5	156	2.41	29.1	44.6	43.‡	170
Pakistan	90.5	44.0	16.9	131	2.96	23.8	49.0	47.0	390
Philippines	52.1	33.9	7.7	59	2.53	27.7	60.9	64.3	760
Singapore	2.5	17.2	5.1	13	1.84	38.0	68.6	73.1	6,620
Sri Lanka	15.4	27.6	7.6	48	1.71	40.9	63.5	66.5	330
Thailand	99.5	31.4	8.4	59	2.31	30.4	59.3	63.2	810
Vietnam	57.2	39.4	12.3	106	2.42	29.0	53.7	58.1	n/a
Oceania:									
Australia	15.4	16.6	7.9	13	1.54	45.4	70.1	77.0	10,780
Fiji	0.7	28.6	4.2	36	1.79	39.1	69.5	73.1	1,790
New Zealand	3.2	17.8	7.9	14	0.52	133.6	69.3	75.7	7,410
Papua New Guinea	3.2	42.5	15.7	111	3.17	22.2	50.5	50.0	790

Source: UN. Statistical offices
Notes: †Official estimate, taking no account of emigration ‡Not revised to take account of latest census *Exc. Taiwan

therefore there is no need to increase manpower. In addition, Singapore's female population has been encouraged to join the workforce because of serious labour shortages and enjoys a freedom and equality unknown in China, where more and more parents, as a result of China's single-child birth control policy, have been aborting unwanted girls, practising infanticide, or crippling girls to gain an allowance for a second, male child. However, although the government programme recommends no more than two children and no financial penalties or stigmas are attached, more and more women are patronising a new clinic which promises to ensure the birth of boys over girls. Similar clinics have opened in Taiwan, South Korea and Malaysia as well.

Overall, it is misleading to interpret high population density as 'crowding', since trade, commerce and industry have mitigated the traditional problems. Based on 1983 estimates, Singapore and Hong Kong show the highest level of GNP per head in the Asian and Pacific regions. However, projections show that, as the population of Asia increases in the future, the supply of productive land will barely increase, leading to ever-expanding food imports.

In general throughout Asia, the age base has shifted to the young because of high fertility and rapidly declining infant mortality. However, in such countries as Japan, the reverse is true: because of low birth rates and extended life expectancy, Japan is the most rapidly ageing country in the world. (See Table 6.2.) By and large the youth group (15–24) is more vocal and critical of its elders, and can be expected to create pressure for radical solution to social inequalities. Expanding secondary and tertiary education has effectively mobilised student protest, which is widespread throughout the region (See Youth unrest.)

In nearly every country of the region, around 80% of the population are located in rural areas. In Peninsular Malaysia and the Philippines, the percentage drops to 70%. In Japan, Australia and New Zealand, the proportions are completely reversed: 75%–90% of the population live in urban areas. Australia leads at 86%, one of the highest levels of urbanisation in the world. In general, outside Japan, urbanisation is proceeding at a faster rate than the growth of employment and is straining the economic and social facilities available. This is all too apparent in the growth of

TABLE 6.2 DISTRIBUTION OF POPULATION BY BROAD AGE GROUPS AND BY RURAL AND URBAN RESIDENCE FOR SELECTED COUNTRIES

mid-1980

	% of total population in the age group			% of total population living in urban or rural areas	
	0–14	15–64	65+	Urban	Rural
Asia:					
Afghanistan	44.2	53.3	2.4	15.6	84.4
Bangladesh	46.2	50.4	3.4	10.4	89.6
Bhutan	40.4	56.4	3.2	3.9	96.1
Burma	41.3	55.0	3.7	27.2	72.8
China (inc. Taiwan)	36.9	58.4	4.7	20.3	79.7
Hong Kong	25.5	68.0	6.5	90.3	9.7
Indonesia (excl. E. Timor)	41.0	55.6	3.3	22.2	77.8
Japan	23.6	67.4	9.0	76.2	23.8
Korea, Dem. People's Republic	40.0	56.3	3.7	59.7	40.3
Korea, Repub.	33.4	62.7	3.9	56.9	43.1
Laos	43.4	53.7	2.9	13.4	86.6
Malaysia	39.1	57.2	3.7	29.4	70.6
Mongolia	43.0	53.8	3.2	52.3	47.7
Nepal	43.5	53.5	3.0	5.0	95.0
Pakistan	45.0	52.1	2.8	28.1	71.9
Philippines	40.6	56.6	2.9	37.4	62.6
Singapore	27.1	68.2	4.7	74.1	25.9
Sri Lanka	36.9	59.0	4.2	21.6	78.4
Thailand	40.2	56.6	3.1	14.4	85.6
Vietnam	41.7	54.6	3.6	19.3	80.7
Oceania:					
Australia	25.6	65.1	9.3	86.3	13.7
Fiji	36.9	60.0	3.1	38.7	61.3
New Zealand	27.1	63.6	9.3	83.3	16.7
Papua New Guinea	42.4	54.3	3.2	13.0	87.0

Source: *UN World Population Prospects: Estimates & Projections as Assessed in 1982 (1985)*

spontaneous slums and shantytowns on the fringes of the large cities. Estimates have been made that one-third of the population of Manila and Seoul lives in squatters' settlements. Jakarta is little better, with one-fifth to one-quarter of the population similarly housed. Singapore and Hong Kong have initiated massive urban re-development projects which have also effectively reduced unemployment through intensive use of labour. According to UN projections, the urban problem is not expected to diminish: by 2000, the number of Asian cities with populations of more than 1 mn will more than double, from 84 to 183.

The numbers of unemployed are also being swelled by the rapid technological change which has been lauded as the region's economic miracle. The rate of industrial growth has been too slow to absorb the population and the excessive introduction of labour-saving devices actually replaces people. Add to this the rising expectations of increasingly educated young people, and you have a recipe for social unrest in the 1990s, when well over another 100 mn will be looking for jobs.

III Trade unionism and labour unrest

Many unions in Asia once had tremendous political clout as leaders of their nations in their struggles for independence. Today, many suffer government repression, limited freedom of association, factionalism, and the slings and arrows of dwindling membership and lacklustre leaders.

In the NICs trade unions have been largely co-opted by government. A high premium is put on industrial peace by these countries and by Japan: they attribute a substantial part of their economic 'miracles' to good labour-management relations.

However, 'good relations' are often more a result of suppression than negotiation. In Singapore, for example, the National Trades Union Congress is virtually an arm of government which puts down any independent action by workers. In Taiwan, though workers can legally set up trade shops, they must be approved by officials of the ruling Kuomintang. In South Korea, labour unions have often been suppressed by military intervention, though the Chun Doo Hwan Government has lately become more flexible, in preparation for the

1988 Olympic Games and in response to threats of aid withdrawal from the United States.

In Hong Kong, gradual reforms in labour legislation have made the government's Labour Department the protector of labour rather than the unions themselves. This has led to a decline in membership. Union membership has also declined in Singapore, where the government, aided by a booming economy, has initiated many wage increases.

Many of these countries would like to emulate Japan in its unique union system, which in effect acts in the interests of management. However, this has failed in Singapore, perhaps due to an absence of company loyalty. But Japan's trades union movement is divided and declining, with membership down to 29.1% in 1984 from a post-World War II peak of 34.4% in 1977. The split falls between Right and Left, and public and private sectors. Japanese unions are also hindered by the fact that they are tied to opposition political parties which have not won an election in post-World War II Japan. More seriously, wages have not kept pace with cost-of-living increases, a trend which appears to be true throughout the region. Some union attempts are being made to gain control over the yearly collective bargaining sessions, or shunto, but this appears to be a long way off.

In South Korea, unionisation has grown with the country's industrial development. The first labour union in South Korea, formed in 1910, catalysed much anti-Japanese activity and the labour movement has remained highly politicised although its ability to act has been constrained by the slow pace of political development: under Chun Doo Hwan it is illegal to hold strikes without government approval. Nevertheless, several strikes have occurred, the most famous at Daewoo Motors in 1984. The Daewoo group chairman personally settled with the young, non-union leaders of the strikes and publicly requested leniency for them. They were sentenced to two years in prison each.

The government has blamed much of the industrial troubles of the past year on activist students, who have been employed, it says, as 'disguised workers' in factories and worked as organisers. In fact the opposition New Korea Democratic Party (NKDP), to which many of the student groups are affiliated, has no formal links with the unions and appears to have no well-thought-out policy on labour.

What is unusual in the South Korean labour movement is that the women, who make up 40% of the workforce, are highly active, and some of the most violent confrontations between labour and police in the country have involved women in the front ranks.

Taiwan has not experienced a major strike since 1949: this can be partly attributed to Taiwan's rapidly-rising wage levels (an average of 16% per year from 1974–1984), coupled with the iron grip maintained by the Kuomintang. That unions play a passive role became all too clear in four mine disasters between 1984 and 1986 which took 277 lives and exposed blatant disregard of safety regulations.

Hong Kong's trade unions are split three ways: pro-China, pro-Taiwan, and independent or moderate. The pro-China, left-wing Hong Kong Federation of Trade Unions (FTU) carries the most weight, with 73 affiliated unions and a declared membership of 166,461. Its chief competition, the right-wing, pro-Taiwan Hong Kong and Kowloon Trades Union Council (TUC) has 71 unions representing 36,564 workers. This has been eroded by the rise of the independents; however, the lack of unity among this group has greatly reduced its influence.

As in South Korea, Malaysia's unions have lost much of the punch they once had in the struggles against Japanese occupation forces and British colonial rule. Leadership and membership patterns have changed to reflect the emerging industrialist society and an independent, Malay-dominated government. Workers' freedom to organise is restricted by the Trade Unions Act of 1959, which gives tremendous discretionary powers to the government Registry of Trade Unions. In addition, the government has used a variety of union-busting techniques, such as not allowing nation-wide unions and mounting anti-union campaigns via missionary groups and political parties. Only about 8.7% of the Malaysian workforce, which totals 5.9 mn, is unionised. This is at least partly because the majority of the free-trade zone (FTZ) workers are not permitted to unionise: in the early 1970s the government attracted foreign investment capital by promising freedom from union disturbances.

In Indonesia as well, the government has gained control over the unions by press-ganging the 21 craft-based unions into 10 'departments' that are more responsive to state direction. Although Indonesian workers are guaranteed by law most basic rights in collective labour practices, they have been too disunited to oppose government moves. The umbrella organisation, which is the All-Indonesia Labour Unions' Federation (FBSI), is dominated by Golkar, a military organisation; and even the state ideology, Pancasila, rejects labour-management confrontation. As a result, even though union leaders say that in reality worker-management relations are as antagonistic as they are in the west, no murmur of dissent is allowed to reach the outside world.

Given their intimate historical ties with Britain, Australia and New Zealand have evolved labour laws and organisations patterned closely after those of the parent country. With strong representation over the years, workers in these countries have steadily achieved huge improvements in wages and working conditions. In Australia, the major emphasis of union campaigns has shifted to superannuation, in the light of an ageing population and severe strains on government welfare spending. Anti-discrimination and equal-opportunity laws are forcing more 'male' jobs open to women as well. But the real battleground has been, and will continue to be for some time to come, structural trends in employment caused by new technologies, shifting international advantage, and factors such as marginal tax rates. In New Zealand, where unions are in transition reflecting the shift from blue-collar to white-collar jobs, Finance Minister Roger Douglas is rapidly liberalising, desubsidising and de-protecting the economy, and the unions are amalgamating in order to exert more influence on government policy.

The Philippines contain what is probably the Pacific Basin's most volatile labour situation, with President Aquino's Government facing 3 mn unemployed and 8 mn underemployed out of a total labour force of 20 mn. Heightened labour militancy is clear from the sharp rise in the number of new labour organisations. There are now 1,960 organisations compared to 1,417 in 1977, with total membership of 4.78 mn. Disunity plagues their ranks and many have refused to register with the Trade Union Congress of the Philippines (TUCP), which acts as a policy-setting advisory body.

TABLE 6.3   UNION STRENGTH

	% workers unionised	Total workforce (million)
Australia	42.0	7.13
Bangladesh[a]	3.0	34.1
Burma	12.2	14.8
China[b]	15.0	530.00
Hong Kong	14.2	2.52
India	4.5	222.5
Indonesia	4.8	63.0
Japan[c]	21.6	57.6
Malaysia	8.7	5.9
New Zealand[d]	52.0	1.37
Pakistan[e]	3.5	28.1
Philippines[h]	24.0	20.0
Singapore	16.0	1.19
South Korea	7.0	14.42
Sri Lanka	30–35	4.5
Taiwan[f]	17.3	7.5
Thailand[g]	1.1	26.6

Notes: [a]Within industrial sector, 26% workers est. organised.

[b]State-owned enterprises employ 100 million workers: 80% are union members.

[c]% unionised increases to 29% when self-employed and families are excluded from workforce.

[d]Unionisable are est. at 800,000 of which 87% are organised.

[e]40% industrial workers est. unionised.

[f]Of 4 million workers with legal right to join unions, 32.5% organised.

[g]6.6% non-agricultural workforce members unionised.

[h]Inc. members of national farmers' organisation.

IV   Youth unrest

Rising expectations coupled with the realities of recession and unemployment and growing anti-American sentiment are creating a climate among Asian youth not unlike that of western youth in the 1960s. In Japan and South Korea, where students constitute a major

116

political force, much of this animus has been directed against the Japanese-US security treaty, against US military bases, and against nuclear weapons in general. In Australia and New Zealand youth groups oppose the testing of French nuclear weapons, and seek to make the Pacific a peace zone. In South Korea and the Philippines, youth protest has been most directly critical of specific leadership and has at times been extremely violent: January-June 1983 saw 128 demonstrations on South Korean campuses crushed by security police.

Governments throughout the region have spearheaded their own youth programmes to co-opt the dissidents. These include the Indonesian National Youth Committee (INYC) which is basically a cultural propaganda organisation; the Kabataang Barangay (KB) in the Philippines, another cultural group which was designed to make youth adopt former President Marcos' New Society Movement, and the Malaysian Islamic Youth Movement, which views Islam as a revolutionary force.

Religion is a particularly strong influence in countries which have large Muslim populations (Indonesia and Malaysia); a characteristic feature of Malaysia's youth movement is its division along national lines as well. The country has an Association of Young Malaysian Chinese, and Congress of Young Malaysian Indians, and a (bumiputra) Student Union of the University of Malaysia. In the Philippines, the Church plays an important role in the ideological training of young people as well. The Philippines has a union of young Christian workers which co-operates with the progressive Democratic Youth Council of the Philippines.

In each country, the youth movements seem at least in part to be alternative tribal systems, as communes were in the 1960s—an attempt to cope with the confusions of rapidly changing times.

117

Chapter Seven

MANUFACTURING IN THE PACIFIC BASIN

The advent of large-scale manufacturing in the Pacific Basin over the last twenty years has not only produced a whole range of economic possibilities for the region. In a real sense, it has completely changed the way that it looks at itself. Manufacturing does not only create self-sufficiency in crucial goods, and generate both the cash and the motivation for domestic development projects; it encourages (indeed, it generally forces) the producer to enter the international markets as a principal agent—instead of merely supplying raw materials on demand from other countries. Manufacturing both complements and confirms the political independence of the country where it goes on—a feature which is observable even in British-ruled Hong Kong.

The close relationship between manufacturing and exporting is perhaps uniquely strong among the Newly Industrialised Countries and the ASEAN members of the Pacific Basin. For more than 20 years the region has based its aggressive growth on the fulfilment of needs both in the Pacific and in North America, and now, with the development of new productive capacity as well as improved communications, it is moving confidently into the European market as well. With its highly-developed entrepreneurial spirit, its stable (if sometimes less than democratic) political structures and its relatively low-waged, placid and easily educated workforce, the Pacific Basin is being seen as a major manufacturing centre in the late 1980s and 1990s.

I Main characteristics of the Pacific manufacturing base

According to the popular image of manufacturing business in the developing countries of South-east Asia, there are two distinct categories of enterprise with relatively little in between. One of these archetypes is the tiny, probably home-based unit, which involves less than 10 people and which relies on the loyalty of a low-paid family and just a handful of people who could be called employees in the true sense. The other is the massive, well-connected, Japanese-style business empire, whose activities are so important to the country that it has actually grown into a channel for the implementation of public policy.

Historically, there has been a fair degree of truth in both images. During the 1960s and 1970s most of the ASEAN countries (South Korea, Malaysia, the Philippines) saw the political usefulness of the large corporations, and helped them grow larger with offers of government contracts. In the Philippines, an additional factor was the quite blatant favouritism showed by President Marcos to his so-called 'cronies'; in South Korea, the six enormous corporations (the *Chaebol*) were ensuring their enduring dominance from the start by feeding back political influence into the government.

In Taiwan, despite the dominant 'small is beautiful' ethic, it was cash from foreign investors (mainly in the United States) which created an industrial elite—although practically the whole manufacturing economy later became mainly home-owned during the increasingly prosperous 1970s, so that nowadays the country makes relatively little provision for foreign ownership in manufacturing. Meanwhile in Hong Kong, many of the major manufacturing corporations have their origins in the trading organisations which found British favour back in the last century.

It was inevitable that the historical pattern of industrial expansion should differ between the primarily commodity-producing countries (Malaysia, Indonesia, Thailand or the Philippines) and those which started out as trading bases (Hong Kong and Singapore). Ports such as Singapore were better known to the developed countries and hence likely to attract foreign investment; they were more likely to have English speakers, or to offer the prospect of an educated workforce; and, above all, they were ideal spots for manufacturing investment because of their access to the trading lanes.

Once in existence, the larger manufacturing organisations rapidly became irreplaceable. By being able to attract the foreign capital essential for national development, they acquired immense political influence on the domestic front; even today, the governments in South Korea or Taiwan dare not annoy the *Chaebols* or their Taiwanese counterparts. In Hong Kong, the hidden political influence of the *Hongs* is undeniable. At the same time, the privileged position of large industries has often helped to ensure that they alone have succeeded in finding the massive investment usually needed for the transition to high-technology manufacturing. Since 1980 many of the major industrial empires in Hong Kong, South Korea and Singapore have further diversified into trading agencies and even investment bankers—all of which has served to strengthen their positions as pillars of the economic community. This divergence in the ability to invest may explain why the balance between large and small manufacturing enterprises has changed relatively little over the years.

TABLE 7.1   MANUFACTURING IN THE PACIFIC ECONOMIES

	Manufacturing as % of GDP		Manufacturing as % of exports
	1965	**1984/5**	**1985**
Industrialised countries			
Japan	42	30	90
NICs			
South Korea	25	30	89
Taiwan	40	80	80
Hong Kong	30	25	72
Singapore	15	24	67
ASEAN			
Indonesia	8	32	6
Malaysia	10	31	25
Philippines	20	26	45
Thailand	14	19	43
Semi-socialist			
Burma	9	9	10

Source: United Nations, National Statistical Agencies

II   Large and small industries in the Pacific Basin

The United Nations Economic and Social Commission for Asia and the Pacific (ESCAP) commented in 1985 that it was very difficult to achieve a true comparison of statistics for the region, because of major differences in the way they are compiled; we might add that subsistence manufacturing, black marketeering and other unseen factors (see Chapter Eight) cloud the crystal ball. But the following attempts to denote the general scale and importance of industry in both NICs and developing ASEAN countries.

Indonesia

In Indonesia, ESCAP thinks that the structure of industry has hardly changed since its last major survey in 1974; then, it found that small-scale and cottage industries (up to four employees) accounted for 99.4% of all enterprises and provided 98% of all employment, but created only 21% of all value-added. Such activities revolve mainly around food-processing and timber-based activities, and are not directly export earners; the gap, then, could scarcely be larger between these and the medium- and large-scale operations which provided 78% of total value-added in 1974, and which included such export commodities as chemical products, plastic and cement products, and electrical appliances.

A major factor in the future of Indonesian manufacturing will be the new oil refineries which have come on stream in the mid-1980s. The potential for a string of downstream industries, including fertiliser manufacture, is clear, and it is likely that the country's larger industries will benefit from more accessible investment capital and a more positive economic climate in which to expand.

Philippines

In the Philippines, there has again been very little change in the industrial structure since the mid-1970s. Small- and medium-sized industries accounted in 1982 for over 90% of all enterprises, employing half the workforce and creating 30% of value-added. Here, their activities include timber and wood processing, engineering goods, textiles and clothing, and food and drink. Large-scale enterprises are largely funded with foreign capital involvement (generally Japanese or American), and include cement, steel, sugar and chemicals, as well as the assembly of televisions and refrigerators from Japanese components. But industry has suffered badly from the turbulence of 1983/85, which made foreign currency expensive to obtain even when it was actually available, and which by devaluing the currency effectively drove the private sector's foreign debts through the roof. In 1987 the Philippines had yet to regain its grace as an investment centre, following the downfall of President Marcos.

Malaysia

A qualitative difference is immediately apparent in Malaysia, where small-scale industries represented only 22.8% of all businesses as long ago as in 1980, although they employed 32% of the workforce. But the small business sector is engaged in such relatively sophisticated activities as construction, light manufacturing, retail trading and wholesaling, which account for 63–74% of its total value-added, employment and fixed assets. Among its larger-scale enterprises, Malaysia has been pushing ahead with its prestige projects (such as the Proton car factory, inaugurated in 1985 in a joint venture with Japan's Mitsubishi). It also has a flourishing trade in televisions, video recorders and most recently microcomputers; the government is developing new industrial estates in the hope of attracting more business away from Japan as the rising value of the yen starts to make Tokyo unattractive to the international markets.

Thailand

In Thailand, the divergence between the very small and the very large manufacturing enterprises is very pronounced. 63.2% of all manufacturing industries are described as cottage industries (up to nine employees), 30.2% as small (10 to 50 employees), 5.3% as medium (51 to 200 employees) and only 1.3% as large (over 200 workers). Yet the large corporations, with their operations in mining, timber and engineering, account for 49.5% of the industrial product and 35.6% of total employment—compared, for example, with 7% and 13.6% for the small and cottage industries (which are mainly in handicrafts).

We may add, incidentally, that this pattern leaves the broad band of medium-scale manufacturers creating over 40% of industrial output. Light engineering, food and timber processing, textiles and other commodity-derived activities dominate the middle sector of the business.

123

Hong Kong

At the other end of the development scale, in Hong Kong, a surprisingly similar industrial structure emerges. 65% of all manufacturing enterprises have less than 10 workers, 15.5% have between 10 and 19, and 11% have between 20 and 49. Thereafter the scale tapers off drastically: only 4.7% employ 50–99 people, 2% employ 100–199, 0.9% 200–499, and 0.2% have between 500 and 999 employees. Altogether the manufacturing sector contributes 24% of Gross Domestic Product, although it provides employment for 35% of the workforce; increasingly important for Hong Kong are the complementary services, financial services and trade.

It is evident, then, that despite the billions of dollars which Hong Kong has ploughed into its heavy industries (steel, chemicals and shipping), the small-scale tailoring, textiles, watch and plastic products industries continue to dominate in the Crown colony. But a telling innovation has been the way that electronics has been following watch manufacture into the small-scale enterprises; as in Taiwan, even quite sophisticated assemblies are being undertaken in what amount to cottage-industry operations. As the necessary manufacturing equipment comes down in price, so the opportunities multiply for the quite extraordinary spirit of enterprise shown by the local population.

South Korea

In South Korea, the dominant role of the half-dozen large-scale enterprises is immediately apparent. They account for 65% of all national output, and they are especially strong in such areas as steel, shipbuilding, television and radio, car manufacture (a notable growth area)—and, most recently, microprocessor manufacturing. But nowadays the drift of government policy is back toward the smaller, more flexible industries, which are expected to raise their share of value-added from 35% in 1981 to 44% by 1991, providing 54% of employment (currently 47%) and 43% of fixed investment (currently 30%).

Singapore

Since the late 1970s, Singapore's manufacturing industry has been moving rapidly away from the traditional labour-intensive activities toward high-technology manufacturing, in accordance with government policy. But there is still no real evidence to suggest that the strategy has paid off, and in the relative stagnation of the mid-1980s the importance of the traditional heavy industries (steel, chemicals, oil refining and engineering) has been appreciated. The oil refining business has taken a knock from the new competition in Indonesia, however.

Pacific Islands

A few of the Pacific islands maintain manufacturing operations, mainly for the substitution of imports, but only Papua New Guinea has broken away to any significant extent from the traditional processing of agricultural raw materials for the domestic market. Its activities include cement manufacturing, steel fabrication, paper products, chemicals and plywood, as well as some light engineering; again unlike its Pacific neighbours, its enterprises are mainly larger than family-sized; 77% of the workforce is engaged by units of more than 20 persons. Nauru and Kiribati were formerly dominated by the phosphate extraction and processing industry, but both have suffered badly from the depletion of reserves and are currently seeking new directions for their stricken economies.

III   The need to export

It seems a curious but inescapable paradox that the future of manufacturing operations in the Pacific Basin should depend so completely on the export market, and not on the needs of their own populations. But, as both ASEAN members and NICs have long realised, there is seldom sufficient purchasing power among domestic consumers to achieve optimum industrial growth. Malaysia has recently confirmed this expectation the hard way, by failing to sell the output from its new prestige car plant on the domestic market, as it had envisaged; in 1987, it is looking to the US consumer to keep its production lines running.

It is not just in the ASEAN countries, either, that domestic demand is insufficient to fuel the growth of industry; in the NICs, and even in well-developed Japan, the relatively simple aspirations of consumers are insufficient to fuel the kind of growth that these companies seek. Wage-earners in Japan and Taiwan save rather than spend their earnings, for a range of cultural and economic reasons; thus it is that the export drive becomes the engine of growth and the arbiter of industrial priorities. Electronic typewriters are utterly unsaleable in Japan and parts of the Pacific Basin where the roman alphabet is not used, but they often figure largely in the industrial drive nevertheless. Much of the Pacific region's clothing production is entirely unsuitable for local wear.

Such examples merely take to extremes a phenomenon which applies to many industries—although most notably in textiles. Often, the important decisions on matters of design, conception and marketing are made from abroad; with a few exceptions the domestic consumer is considered last of all. In such cases, particularly for luxury goods, he may account for less than a quarter of total sales.

Historically, cheap labour has been the key to the Asian NICs' success in overseas sales, but often the competitive advantage is compounded by other factors. An undervalued currency may make the products easier to sell abroad. Another advantage, in the case of steel and cement, is that the goods are being produced near to their destination markets. In the case of petroleum products, the Gulf War between Iran and Iraq has made Japan look for supplies outside the war zone—such as Indonesia's new refining capability.

A weak currency has been a major reason why South Korea's shipbuilding industry is one of the few to be making money anywhere in the world. The won/dollar exchange rate slid by nearly 80% between 1980 and 1986, making a decisive difference at a time when the world market was tight. In the case of steel, the ASEAN countries gained from having new plant based on modern electric-arc continuous casting systems, in contrast to many of their cumbersome competitors in Europe and the United States.

Taiwan has clearly proved that it is possible to combine high technology with low industrial wages. The steady, persevering work ethic and the preference for clearly established authority structures are conducive to an intensive, cost-effective manufacturing operation with relatively few industrial labour troubles.

126

IV   The threat from new technology

It is too early in 1987 to rule out a new and rather startling possibility for the region: that new technology may yet swing the global cost advantage back towards producers in Japan and the United States, even in the kind of basic products where the developing countries of South-east Asia currently lead the way. Computerised textile looms are now capable of replacing almost the entire workforce, and produce cloth both uniformly and to a high standard. Laser-beam technology is being applied to the manufacture of plywood and veneers, resulting in higher-strength and better-quality products. Shipbuilding benefits from the use of high-powered computer systems which take much of the guesswork out of ship design.

Another significant change for industry is likely to come in the steel foundry business. Instead of manufacturing steel in bulk and selling from stock, Japan is investing in new computerised plant which will allow it to produce limited-volume consignments of special steels, each batch tailored precisely to the customer's requirements. It was only as recently as 1980 that Japan pioneered the low-inventory, manufactured-to-order industrial principle which has gained increasing popularity since then in Europe and the United States—but which will be less easy to implement in a lower-technology environment, or where communications are anything less than perfect.

It is far from clear in the mid-1980s whether any of the Asian NICs, let alone the ASEAN developing states, can match this kind of technological advantage without massive industrial investment. Without it, they could perhaps lose their current competitive edge in these kinds of products. Assuming that they cannot develop such technologies themselves, they will have to look abroad for funding, and perhaps for equity involvement—and it will be essential to gain the confidence of foreign investors at a time when trade tensions are sharpening.

V   Pacific Basin manufacturing in a world context

The following section aims to illustrate some of the issues

confronting the Pacific Basin as a whole, and to cast light on the way in which shifting world trends have affected its members. As far as possible, it tries to stay above the specific differences between one country and another.

It will be clear, of course, that the NICs have a somewhat better chance than their ASEAN neighbours in adapting to the pressures of change; but what their industries gain from being independent of commodity price developments, they are liable to lose because of increased competition from Japan on the world markets.

Food processing

As the region's industrial base continues to gain in confidence and sophistication, the role played by food processing has been falling away quite sharply. In 1986, however, two years of shrinkage ended with an estimated 4.6% growth—but this was still less than half the growth rate of the early 1980s. Food processing contributes less than 7% to South Korea's industrial output, whereas it continues to account for around 40% of business in Indonesia. Indonesia and South Korea are important cigarette producers, and Malaysia, the Philippines and Thailand produce significant quantities of smoking tobacco, mainly for regional markets.

Textiles and clothing

Textiles and clothing continue to be a major source of income for the region, and the industry has been growing at between 4 and 6% a year since the early 1980s—with the notable exception of 1985, when output actually fell by 2.8% amid the economic doubts which accompanied the slowing of growth in the all-important US market. In 1982 the region recorded a $3 bn surplus in textiles alone. The clothing business is heavily concentrated in South Korea and Hong Kong, which with China accounted for 75% of the developing world's clothing exports in 1984; of this figure, 60% was sold to the United States.

Leather processing has suffered somewhat from the use of leather substitutes in developed-country shoe manufacturing, but Taiwan, Hong Kong and South Korea have moved energetically into such new markets as leather fashion wear. Leather shoes in these

128

countries are directed at the domestic market, but all three have compensated admirably in the world market for sports and canvas shoes, where they enjoy a significant cost advantage over European or American competitors.

Wood products

Plywood and similar products are important to Indonesia, Malaysia and the Philippines, which provide two-thirds of the United States' imports. Japan imported $5.3 bn worth of timber in 1984, of which saw timber and plywood comprised 16%. Most of the region maintains a ban on exporting raw logs, preferring to process its timber in its own sawmills. Furniture manufacturing in the region is dominated by the Philippines, which exports $50 mn worth a year to the United States, and increasingly by Taiwan. Both countries concentrate particularly on chipboard and veneer manufacture.

Paper

All Pacific Basin countries (including also most of Indochina) are currently investing in new paper and pulp making plant, in a renewed effort to satisfy domestic demand. Indonesia, which imported 40% of its requirements as recently as 1984, has since then built two newsprint plants, a new pulp mill and a kraft paper factory. South Korea raised its output by nearly 30% between 1983 and 1986. The printing and publishing business itself has been growing at around 5% a year, although 1985 was a highly disappointing year with growth of only 1%. It is no coincidence that publishing is concentrated in Hong Kong and Singapore; good communications and a high level of capital investment are essential as new technology strengthens its hold on the business.

Chemicals

South-east Asia has one of the world's highest growth rates in industrial chemicals, at around 9% in 1986, but the trend is currently downward. This is partly due to falling prices which resulted from the oil glut of the mid-1980s, but it also reflects the increasing impact of Saudi Arabia's massive new plants (opened in 1984/85). Nonetheless, UNIDO expects to see a 3–4% annual

129

growth in the developing countries' own consumption of these goods, especially fertilisers and pesticides.

Pharmaceuticals

Pharmaceuticals are especially important in South Korea, where they comprised 54% of non-industrial chemical production in 1980, and in the Philippines where they represented 49%. However, this side of the industry is heavily controlled by multinational corporations, which alone can fund the costly research on which they depend.

Petrochemicals

With the opening of its new refineries, Indonesia now accounts for half the region's petroleum products. As already noted, the sector has been blighted by a slow rate of increase in demand, and since 1985 by generally poor international prices. Nevertheless, exploration for new resources continues at a rapid pace. Plastics production is expected to grow by around 7% per annum in the late 1980s, as demand in developing countries (especially China) continues to grow. But rubber products, once the mainstay of Malaysia's economy, have been hit by the recession and over-supply in the world motor tyre industry, and by substitution in several high-technology products.

Building materials

There is still investment in building materials, which expect to continue their growth in the late 1980s despite the construction slump in Singapore. Cement is likely to be in strong demand, especially from China, which may take up some of the slack left by the construction slump in Singapore.

Metals

It is doubtful in 1987 whether steel production will ever re-attain the 20% growth rates of the 1970s; all over the world, demand has been hit by substitution with other substances—and simply by the increased efficiency and economy with which the metal is employed. As has already been noted, developed countries may regain their competitive edge with new production technologies which may make the region's plants look obsolete before long.

130

Much of the region has been investing in new smelting plant which would enable it to process its own output of non-ferrous metals. But the continuing slump in markets for copper, tin and lead have conspired against further expansion, which will have to await a revival of international prices.

Non-electrical machinery

Although well behind such competitors as India and Mexico, the South-east Asian nations are important contributors to the non-electrical machinery business (engines, agricultural machinery, metal and woodworking machinery, office and computing equipment). Apart from computers and office equipment, much of the output is destined for the domestic market, which is certain to increase as the region continues to develop. Except perhaps in Taiwan, the sector is especially dependent on foreign capital, much of which derives from Japan in the form of joint-venture operations.

Electronics

As long ago as 1980, electronics represented 80% of the electrical goods industry in Malaysia, 75% in Singapore and 68% in South Korea. Of the three, only South Korea manufactures a significant proportion of its own components, and all three export the greater part of their output. As production facilities in South-east Asia have grown more sophisticated, electronics companies in Europe and the United States have increasingly tended to transfer their production to the region. Nonetheless, the industry is surprisingly vulnerable to short-term fluctuations, and output fell in 1985 by some 5% before staging a limited resurgence in 1986.

TABLE 7.2 DEVELOPMENT OF INDUSTRIAL AND MANUFACTURING SECTORS, 1975–1984

Base: 1980=100

	1976	1978	1980	1982	1984	1985
Australia						
General	92	94	100	90	—	—
Manufacturing	93	94	100	88	—	—
Power and water	79	87	100	106	—	—

131

TABLE 7.2 DEVELOPMENT OF INDUSTRIAL AND MANUFACTURING SECTORS, 1975–1984 *(continued)*

Base: 1980=100

	1976	1978	1980	1982	1984	1985
Fiji						
General	—	91	100	109	116	158
Gold mining	—	114	100	186	196	136
Manufacturing	—	91	100	109	116	162
Power and water	—	94	100	108	143	138
Indonesia						
Mining	95	102	100	85	89	85
Manufacturing	56	75	100	110	123	—
Japan						
General	80	89	100	101	117	125
Mining	102	107	110	96	96	96
Manufacturing	80	89	100	101	117	126
Chemicals	78	92	100	102	118	126
Non-electric machinery	70	81	100	101	113	130
Electrical machinery	63	76	100	125	194	220
Transport equipment	79	80	100	99	104	109
South Korea						
General	62	91	100	118	154	163
Mining	91	101	100	97	104	110
Manufacturing	61	91	100	119	158	167
Textiles	66	81	100	114	124	121
Clothing	73	102	100	123	150	160
Wood and furniture	106	145	100	120	159	130
Paper and products	56	82	100	118	142	145
Non-electric machinery	82	133	100	141	244	280
Electrical machinery	56	99	100	128	230	254
Transport equipment	53	111	100	163	273	280
Electricity	62	85	100	116	144	160
Malaysia*						
General	73	87	100	109	142	139
Mining	103	102	100	104	163	161
Manufacturing	71	86	100	109	130	134
Electricity	67	82	100	110	133	151
Philippines						
General	80	90	100	110	—	—

TABLE 7.2   DEVELOPMENT OF INDUSTRIAL AND MANUFACTURING
SECTORS, 1975–1984 *(continued)*

Base: 1980=100

	1976	1978	1980	1982	1984	1985
Mining	69	91	100	112	95	—
Manufacturing	82	91	100	112	95	
Electricity	69	81	100	117	130	—
Singapore						
Manufacturing	—	78	100	104	103	103
Clothing	—	100	100	92	103	102
Chemicals	—	91	100	119	230	—
Household electrical and						
industrial equipment	—	63	100	116	95	—
Electrical equipment	—	61	100	94	110	114
Transport equipment	—	63	100	112	120	105

Source: United Nations
Note: *Peninsular Malaysia only

VI   Funding industrial expansion

The mid-1980s have seen a drastic change in the way the business
world goes about raising its development funding. As the heady
days of international syndicated loans have evaporated in the 1980s,
their place has been taken by the all-pervading 'securitisation' of
corporate finance, in which companies cease to depend on the
centralised channels of government for their expansion, but instead
branch out on their own with issues of shares, bonds and
commercial paper of all descriptions. In 1986 the total volume of the
old-fashioned internationally syndicated loans was no more than
half that of 1980, while the volume of corporate securities had
increased perhaps fourfold. As described in Chapter 5, this suits the
international banks very well: after the series of near-defaults by
debtor nations in the early 1980s, they are in no hurry to take
further risks without receiving some sort of security in exchange for
their money, and the equity business is the obvious way to go about it.

We have already seen that further industrial expansion is

133

desirable for most of the Pacific region, and that such industries as textiles, electronics (in South Korea), shipbuilding and wood processing may well founder without it. For the developing countries in the region, the future of the manufacturing base will therefore depend to quite a large extent on how successful they are in adjusting to these new conditions. Leaving aside Taiwan (which nowadays could, but does not, export capital), these countries will continue to need industrial funding from abroad—particularly where they are vulnerable to the impact of new technological developments.

Progress is often slow in adapting to the new international environment, however. In several South-east Asian countries (South Korea, Thailand, and especially Taiwan) there are steep barriers against direct foreign equity investment which are only slowly coming down. An important force for change in the next five years will be the growth of the global securities market, which will both encourage East Asia's corporate borrowers to look to Wall Street or Tokyo for their money, and which will at the same time bind them more tightly into the international business community. Since 1985 South Korea has opened up four rather generalised funds to foreigners (although it still bars direct personal investment), and even China has been looking for ways to raise money through international bonds. Progress in Taiwan has been promised, but it has been very slow in coming.

VII The drift towards the private sector

Many of the non-socialist Asian countries of the Pacific Basin are in the fortunate position of having largely completed the basic infrastructural phase of their economic development; that is to say, their industrial estates, their steelworks, concrete plants, major roads and communications facilities (except, usually, railways) are fairly well developed. They have thus reached the point where the private manufacturing sector is well placed to take over the task of further industrial development from their respective central governments, and all of this makes it easier to attract foreign money. The process of privatising state-owned industries is gathering pace in Malaysia, Thailand and Indonesia, as well as in South Korea where it is quite well advanced.

VIII   Japan as an exporter of industrial capital

Japan, as explained in Chapter Five, is fortunate in having an unusually resourceful domestic capital market. Private saving levels are high, and the financial structure is one of the largest (though certainly not the most sophisticated) in the world.

Japan has always been active in promoting the industrial development of its Pacific neighbours, but the level of its direct foreign investment has risen steeply since the early 1980s—especially in low-wage economies such as South Korea, Taiwan and the Philippines. But in addition to its old hunting grounds in the ASEAN countries and the NICs, Tokyo is looking increasingly to the mass market in China, where potential consumption of vehicles, chemicals and electrical equipment is vast. It has also offered industrial assistance to several Pacific islands (including Vanuatu, Kiribati and Fiji), because it says the reduction of American assistance is opening the door to the Soviet Union in the region.

In fact, its motives are everywhere more transparent. The huge expansion of the Japanese trade surplus is creating problems of its own; not only is it impossible to invest it all on the sluggish domestic market, but it is attracting international condemnation because it sucks resources away from the countries which have still to attain developed-country status. Japan's very large trade surplus with all the ASEAN and NICs is the most convincing reason why its capital involvement in the region's manufacturing sector will continue to grow in the next five years.

Chapter Eight

TRADE IN THE PACIFIC BASIN

I Introduction

Chapter Seven has already demonstrated the dominant role of foreign trade in the development of the manufacturing industry in the Pacific Basin; but the international involvement of the region has traditionally been based not on manufactures but on commodities and semi-processed goods. For many of these countries, particularly the ASEAN group (but excluding Singapore), such relatively un-refined activities still make up the bulk of exports in the late 1980s.

In the twentieth century, the main function of export industries in the Pacific Basin has been to fill in the gaps left by such developed countries as Japan and the United States, its main trading partners. As Japan became a high-wage economy, its low-wage manufacturing functions were assumed by Hong Kong, Taiwan, South Korea and Singapore, and its raw material needs were met by the ASEAN partners Thailand, Indonesia, the Philippines and Malaysia; as each of these countries in turn developed it became possible to establish the organised, powerful and increasingly high-technology industries which mark out the Asian NICs (Hong Kong, South Korea, Singapore and Taiwan) in the mid-1980s. Meanwhile the ASEAN countries were themselves moving slowly toward industrialised status, through such activities as electronics in Malaysia and oil refining in Indonesia. All of these activities, including Malaysia's latest prestige motor manufacturing project, are aimed at foreign markets.

Thus, in the space of barely twenty years the region has had to develop and then discard one industrial stage after another, and at each stage it has been the export potential rather than the domestic demand which has determined the next step. The region's ratio of exports to Gross Domestic Product is well above 50%—rising to 80% in Singapore and Hong Kong if services exports are included. These figures compare with 13% in Japan, for example, and only 5.4% in the United States.

1987 has brought a further sharpening of the economic imbalances between Japan and the United States, as the two countries have engaged in mutual recriminations over the relative strengths of their currencies and especially over the Japanese trade surplus with Washington. Unfortunately the worsening atmosphere between these two giants has led each of them into rather generalised and indiscriminate protectionism against imports, and the result has caught the Pacific Basin countries in the middle as they try to sell to both markets. At the same time the collapse of the international commodity markets in the early 1980s has removed the safety net for such countries as Malaysia, Indonesia and the Philippines, and this has added an unwelcome element of risk to the whole business. In the Philippines, political uncertainties have been compounded by shortages of foreign exchange.

Fortunately no such worries have been apparent so far in Hong Kong, which is due to revert to Chinese sovereignty in 1997. This is partly because the Communist Government in Beijing has been giving strong signals that it will not seek to communalise the local economy; indeed, it is positively eager to take advantage of Hong Kong's trading expertise. Nonetheless, we may expect some nervousness among the resident community as the deadline approaches in the next decade.

TABLE 8.1   EXPORT DEVELOPMENT IN THE PACIFIC BASIN, 1970–1985

All exports: annual growth rate (%)

	1970–79	1979–81	1982	1983	1984	1985
NICs	28.5	19.2	− 1.1	8.2	20.1	5.0
Hong Kong	22.1	19.9	− 3.7	4.6	29.0	6.2
South Korea	37.9	18.9	2.6	9.1	19.6	8.8
Singapore	28.0	19.3	− 0.9	5.0	10.2	− 4.0
Taiwan	30.8	18.7	− 2.3	13.6	21.3	2.0
ASEAN	26.2	15.0	− 4.1	0.1	9.4	0.0
Indonesia	34.9	23.6	− 6.2	− 5.3	3.4	3.0
Malaysia	23.3	3.1	2.3	17.4	15.3	− 1.0
Philippines	17.6	11.5	−12.3	− 1.8	9.1	− 2.4
Thailand	25.2	15.1	− 1.2	−11.3	16.1	10.3

TABLE 8.1   EXPORT DEVELOPMENT IN THE PACIFIC BASIN, 1970–1985
(continued)

All exports: annual growth rate (%)						
	1970–79	1979–81	1982	1983	1984	1985
South Asia	15.7	7.4	1.5	8.3	—	—
Other NICs	20.1	13.2	− 5.5	3.7	—	—
World	20.6	10.0	− 7.2	− 2.4	—	—

Manufactured exports: annual growth rate (%)		
	1970–79	1979–81
NICs	29.7	19.8
Hong Kong	22.0	19.5
South Korea	39.2	18.6
Singapore	33.0	20.8
Taiwan	34.2	20.7
ASEAN	39.4	15.5
Indonesia	47.4	28.1
Malaysia	38.0	9.0
Philippines	33.8	17.0
Thailand	47.1	20.0
South Asia	17.2	—
Other NICs	24.1	23.7
World	19.7	17.4

Sources: UN/IMF/OECD/National accounts/*ASEAN Economic Bulletin*

II   The international context: dependence on a seesawing trade climate

It will be immediately clear from the accompanying tables how much the Pacific region owes to Japan and the United States; in 1986, as usual, the two countries consumed almost half of its total exports. But Tables 8.2 and 8.3 illustrate quite clearly the way in which both the NICs and the ASEAN group have been forced over the last 15 years to zigzag between the two countries in their efforts to maximise the benefits to their economies. The reason lies in the quite different characters of these two key economies, and in the different way that they react to specific external conditions.

139

TABLE 8.2   DIRECTION OF EXPORTS

Destinations, as % of total exports

Asian NICs (including Singapore)	1970	1979	1981	1983
NICs	7.8	8.7	9.9	7.9
ASEAN	10.2	9.4	10.3	12.2
South Asia	0.8	2.5	3.0	3.1
Middle East	1.5	5.7	5.9	6.2
Other Less Developed Countries	10.0	7.6	9.8	9.6
Japan	11.7	13.1	10.4	9.1
USA	31.8	26.5	25.9	31.5
Australia	2.3	2.5	2.7	2.2
EEC	15.0	16.2	13.1	10.9
Other Developed Countries	7.0	6.0	4.9	4.7
Total Pacific	63.8	62.7	59.2	62.9
Total Less Developed Countries	30.3	33.9	38.9	39.0
Total Developed Countries	67.8	64.3	57.0	58.4

Sources: IMF/UN/OECD/National accounts/*ASEAN Economic Bulletin*

TABLE 8.3   GENERAL DIRECTION OF EXPORTS

Destinations, as % of total exports

ASEAN, excluding Singapore	1970	1979	1981	1983
NICs	18.9	17.8	17.8	21.0
ASEAN	5.2	3.1	3.6	3.9
South Asia	0.6	1.3	1.6	1.7
Middle East	1.2	1.6	2.3	2.0
Other Less Developed Countries	1.8	3.3	5.9	4.8
Japan	28.4	33.1	32.7	30.3
USA	19.6	19.3	17.7	18.7
Australia	1.8	1.4	1.8	1.2
EEC	15.4	14.5	11.3	11.0
Other Developed Countries	3.1	2.3	2.2	2.4
Total Pacific	73.9	76.0	73.7	75.1
Total Less Developed Countries	27.7	27.1	31.2	33.4
Total Developed Countries	68.4	70.6	65.7	63.7

Sources: IMF/UN/OECD/National accounts/*ASEAN Economic Bulletin*

III Japan

The most fundamental of all economic factors for Japan is its complete dependence on imports of fuel and other mineral resources. The industrial expansion of the 1960s and 1970s was built very largely on supplies of iron, rubber, copper, coal and later petroleum from what are now the ASEAN countries, as well as low-technology manufactures from the NICs. Sales of textiles and clothing were, and still are, a major source of revenue to the region's developing economies; as Tables 8.4 and 8.5 show, foodstuffs and textile products are still the most popular of Japan's purchases from the region.

With its extreme dependence on imported oil, Japan suffered a severe loss of confidence after the first oil shock of 1973/75. But it made a rather better recovery than its competitors in the industrialised world, and the rapid resumption of purchasing proved to be an important factor in the subsequent development of the region. Still, as the late 1970s progressed, the balance shifted on the supply side with the more intensive industrialisation of Hong Kong and the shift in Singapore toward higher value-added manufacturing. The result was that Japan, with its own thriving manufacturing sector, became less attracted to the region's products, preferring to sponsor their entry to the world markets via a series of joint ventures in the NICs.

Japan has been less successful in pulling away from the effects of the world recession which followed the second oil shock in 1979. Despite a thriving external sector, the domestic scene has remained stubbornly resistant to all stimuli from the central government—for example, a low bank rate, which ought to have boosted consumption and investment.

The impact on Pacific trade has been twofold. Firstly, Tokyo's purchases of raw materials and other goods from both ASEAN and the NICs have remained relatively subdued—except, that is, for petroleum, now that the Gulf War between Iran and Iraq has disrupted its traditional supplies from the Middle East, diverting its buyers to Singapore and more recently Indonesia. Secondly, Japan has been forced to turn more and more of its production toward the external markets, where its goods (electronics, motor vehicles, textiles and sometimes steel) now compete head-on with cars,

141

computers and audio equipment from the NICs. Only in clothing is there no real challenge at present.

IV The United States

If Japan had difficulty getting out of the post-oil shock slump in the early 1980s, the opposite was true for the region's other main trading partner, the United States. From late 1982 to the end of 1985, the US economy made colossal strides under the policies of President Reagan, borrowing freely so as to foster an abnormally high rate of domestic growth. The result (rather paradoxically, in view of the steep budget and current account deficits) was a severe overvaluation of the US dollar, which lasted until mid-1985 and which allowed both the developing ASEAN countries and the NICS to boost their sales to this buoyant US market.

Alas, it also created resentment among American producers, who found themselves underpriced not only on international markets but on their home ground. Since 1984 this resentment has led to increasing pressures within the USA for restrictive import policies; the subsequent fall of the dollar, making America's imports more expensive, has done little to quell the demands from those who have recently seen the US economy pausing for breath.

In fact, as Table 8.7 shows, the American boom for ASEAN and NIC producers was already slowing by early 1985 and was in any case nowhere near as pronounced as Washington has maintained. Indeed, only Indonesia and Taiwan (which is not listed in the table) appear to have increased their US sales at the particular expense of, say, Japan during this period. The pressure ought to have eased again in 1986, as the rise in the Japanese yen increased the potential for Pacific Basin sales to Tokyo and simultaneously depressed the appetite for imports in the USA.

The region's sales to the US have been particularly marked in a handful of specialist sectors. The sports shoe business is a case in point, being practically dominated in the USA by South Korean and Taiwanese manufacturers who take advantage of lower wage costs. The South Korean car manufacturer Hyundai has made considerable inroads into the US market for specialist and off-road vehicles, and audio and TV equipment (often made under licence from Japanese companies) is now well established in the US marketplace.

Recently, America has itself added to the flow of goods from the region. Increasingly, American high-technology companies such as Apple and even IBM have been diverting quite large parts of their own production to South Korea, Taiwan and Malaysia, in a concerted and generally successful effort to reduce their US costs.

V Growing pains: the Newly Industrialised Countries

Taiwan, Hong Kong, Singapore and South Korea are without doubt the fastest growing of the manufacturing nations in the Pacific region. Each of the 'four little dragons' owes it success in large part to a vigorous development of its export markets, especially in the United States. Each is producing far more than it can consume, and as such depends on the health of its external economy. But none has been exempt from the pressures imposed on the free market by protectionist sentiment, both in Japan and in the United States.

Hong Kong, the oldest of the four, has been a trading port since the earliest days of British rule. Its traditional clothing exports still comprised 34.6% of its foreign sales in 1985, despite the emergence of electronics (14.8%) and the continued importance of clocks and watches (7.1%) and toys (also 7.1%). But the colony has suffered badly from the contraction of the US market; such was its dependence on exports that a 5% fall in real exports during 1985 was sufficient to brake its economic growth from 9.3% (1984) to only 0.8%.

Even so, 44.5% of Hong Kong's exports went to the USA in 1985, while the UK absorbed only 6.6%. By far the fastest growing export customer was China, whose purchases rose by 35% to account for a surprising 12% of its total sales. Only 3.4% of all Hong Kong's exports were sold to Japan, reflecting perhaps the extent to which the two countries' manufacturing industries overlap.

In addition to its HK $129,880 mn worth of exports (1985), the colony has a thriving entrepôt trade with China and the United States. The Beijing market alone was worth HK $46,000 mn in 1985,

and this can be expected to rise substantially in the near future—
together, we should add, with a major flow of services to the
mainland Chinese.

Singapore has traditionally made more of its national income
from entrepôt activities than from exporting its domestically-
produced goods, but the last five years have seen the balance shift
back toward domestic sales. There has been a boom in sales of
computers, office equipment and other electronic products as the
country's commitment to high skills, high value-added and high
technology has taken shape; in 1985 these accounted for more than
a third of all exports. Meanwhile there is plenty of export activity in
plastics, one of the region's principal growth areas, and in
chemicals. But Singapore no longer exports the labour-intensive
goods which were its staple products only ten years ago, and it has
lost much of its ship repairing and oil rig construction business due
to market contraction.

Most of Singapore's imports are brought in without quotas or
other restrictions, and are re-exported free of duty under the
country's entrepôt facilities. The character of such re-exports has
changed drastically in the last decade, with crude rubber representing
only 12% of the total in 1985, compared with 36% in 1975.

There is also rapid change as far as true exports are concerned.
Machinery and equipment comprised a third of the 1985 total, with
petroleum products providing another 32.8% and other manufactures 7.1%. There has been a pronounced dip in the volume and
value of petroleum products exported from Singapore since 1984,
when Indonesia entered the contest with the inauguration of its new
refineries.

Difficult export markets in the United States only added to
Singapore's problems. In 1985 demand from the USA grew by only
3% in nominal terms, to comprise just 21.2% of Singapore's foreign
sales—compared, for example, with 50% in 1983. Next in importance
was neighbouring Malaysia, which accounted for 14.4%; Japan,
with 9.4%; and Hong Kong with 6.4%.

Taiwan enjoys the closest links with the USA of all the Asian
NICs, and it has managed to keep its US business on an even keel

even in the face of rising protectionism in that country. It recorded a $10,000 mn trade surplus with the US in 1985, and around $12,000 mn in 1986, exporting mainly electronics, textiles and clothing. (This, it might be added, is equivalent to a per capita surplus of more than $600 in US trade alone—a sum which could settle the $10,000 mn foreign debt in the space of just ten months).

The falling price of raw material inputs and the low level of foreign debt have combined to place Taiwan in a unique trading position. With foreign currency reserves of some $23,000 mn in 1986, the strength of its currency has become a positive embarrassment and a real hindrance to trade with the other Asian nations— meaning in effect that it has become more dependent on the USA's custom than it would have wished.

Washington has never seriously expected Taiwan's 20 mn inhabitants to buy enough US goods to restore the trade balance, but it has become seriously annoyed at Taipei's imposition of countervailing duties on American electronics, tobacco and drinks, and especially on textiles; in retaliatory mood, it has cut its own import quotas for Taiwanese textiles in favour of Hong Kong, which as a freeport does not levy such tariffs on American goods.

Careful study of Taiwan's trade patterns reveals that Washington's dollars are ultimately finishing up in Japan and Saudi Arabia. The USA bought 48.1% of Taiwan's exports in 1985, but supplied only 23% of its imports. Japan, on the other hand, ran a large surplus with Taipei by supplying 27.6% of its import requirements while buying only 11.3% of its exports. Hong Kong purchased 8.3% of exports but supplied only 1.6% of all imports, and Singapore bought 2.9% while delivering a mere 1.4% of its imports. Finally, Saudi Arabian oil accounted for 6.8% of the import bill while the Saudis bought only 1.9% of all exports.

With its highly restrictive rules on foreign currency and foreign capital transactions, Taiwan is only marginally in the market for regional investment projects among the other Asian NICs or the ASEAN nations. The lack of foreign contact at this level has helped foster a surprisingly insular outlook, which in time may prove an obstacle to the much-needed but often ignored renovation of industrial plant in Taiwan.

145

In short, it seemed in early 1987 as though Taiwan was being lured into a corner by its own trading success. The effective slide in the currency's value, as detailed below, seems to reflect an effort to redress the balance in favour of trade within the area, but it is at best only a tentative move toward the extensive change of attitude which will be required if it is to integrate fully into the regional trade pattern.

TABLE 8.4 EXPORTS FROM NICs, ACCORDING TO COMMODITY AND DESTINATION

**Distribution of total exports
in each community category, by destination**

Destination:	NICs		ASEAN		Japan		USA		EEC	
	1970	1981	1970	1981	1970	1981	1970	1981	1970	1981
Raw materials	8.4	16.5	11.6	22.5	22.2	18.7	7.9	8.3	14.4	4.7
Clothing	0.7	0.9	1.1	0.2	7.0	8.3	48.5	39.5	26.3	10.3
Electrical machinery	9.1	11.1	3.9	7.4	5.3	5.1	61.9	39.0	10.3	16.0
Miscellaneous manufactures	3.8	4.6	3.4	3.1	3.7	5.8	58.2	40.9	15.2	23.9
Textiles	20.5	23.4	12.7	8.2	5.6	10.2	12.4	7.7	16.2	7.5
Agricultural and food products	7.3	9.6	15.9	10.9	23.5	31.0	14.2	11.5	18.4	7.4
Resource-based manufactures	5.0	9.0	7.6	6.2	15.9	8.8	40.2	22.4	7.9	13.8
Non-electrical machinery	8.6	6.8	45.6	23.1	5.2	5.8	20.7	29.8	4.0	7.6
Manufactured exports	7.5	8.6	8.9	7.5	7.1	6.9	41.2	31.9	14.3	15.8

Source: United Nations/*ASEAN Economic Bulletin*

VI Past, present and future for the ASEAN nations

The Association of South East Asian Nations has always had a major role to play in the development of foreign trade among its three mainly commodity-based members, Malaysia, Thailand and the Philippines, and its relatively industrialised states, Singapore and more recently South Korea. (Brunei, with its extraordinary oil-derived wealth, is the Association's sixth member, but its advanced state of development places it outside the scope of most ASEAN co-operation projects.) ASEAN serves both as a forum for mutual assistance, co-ordinating the positioning and sometimes the funding of key regional projects, and as a kind of common market with preferential tariffs and some standardisation of trade procedures.

In the mid-1980s most of the region is regarded as middle-income for trade purposes; that is to say, it no longer enjoys such preferential treatment as hitherto in matters of trade under the United States' Generalised System of Preferences, and it no longer attracts so many soft loans from the World Bank and other multilateral agencies. But this is amply compensated by the influx of foreign companies who see these budding NICs as a springboard for new trade ventures in the Pacific region.

Since 1979 the ASEAN group has sought closer trading links with the European Community, and regular ministerial links have been maintained to this end. As Tables 8.5 and 8.7 indicate, however, direct trade with western Europe declined somewhat in 1981–1983, before staging a rather patchy comeback in 1984–1985 (most notably in South Korea, as its electronics industries gained influence).

Relations with Japan have been marked by complaints that Tokyo is using both its formal trade tariffs and its notorious 'non-tariff barriers' to keep out ASEAN's manufactured products. Over 90% of the region's sales to Tokyo are in the form of raw materials, whereas about 90% of its purchases from that country are manufactured products: engineering, transport goods, electronics and so forth. Japan has responded since 1985 with tariff concessions, and has intensified its industrial investment in ASEAN in an attempt to rectify the long-term imbalances.

In fact the ASEAN group has historically sold more to Japan than it buys. But the $8,300 mn trade surplus of 1979 had shrunk to $4,600 mn by 1983, and preliminary figures for 1985 suggest that the sum was nearing a balance. A few countries are quite heavily in debt to Japan: South Korea, for example, had a $3,000 mn deficit in 1985 which it could ill afford, and for Singapore the figure was nearly

$5,000 mn. Only Malaysia and (increasingly) Indonesia are managing to maintain a trade surplus with Tokyo.

ASEAN's relations with the United States have also been stormy at times. In February 1985 the US Special Trade Representative William Brock visited an ASEAN summit in Kuala Lumpur to receive a full-frontal attack from the organisation's members for his country's policies toward the region. Top of the list of complaints were the USA's imposition of countervailing duties against ASEAN exports; the high prevailing level of US interest rates, which were felt to be subduing American investment; and the US tariff restrictions on ASEAN shipping. As a whole, the region has seen its sales to the USA decline in real terms since 1980; especially affected have been textiles and clothing, food products and resource-based

TABLE 8.5   EXPORTS FROM ASEAN COUNTRIES, BY COMMODITY AND DESTINATION

**Distribution of total exports
in each commodity category, by destination**

Destination:	NICs		ASEAN		Japan		USA		EEC	
	1970	1981	1970	1981	1970	1981	1970	1981	1970	1981
Raw materials	18.7	16.9	5.5	2.7	36.4	44.9	13.5	16.2	13.0	6.5
Clothing	6.0	5.1	7.9	0.4	—	2.3	66.0	29.2	—	36.4
Electrical machinery	30.3	33.9	13.4	3.6	—	3.9	—	44.8	—	11.4
Miscellaneous manufactures	41.2	17.1	13.2	2.3	8.1	5.9	15.9	33.4	11.1	24.5
Textiles	31.1	25.0	11.0	5.2	10.3	10.7	17.8	11.8	12.7	18.7
Agricultural and food products	17.8	15.1	3.8	6.3	11.7	11.8	34.5	12.3	21.5	22.6
Resource-based manufactures	13.1	27.9	3.3	4.4	8.6	8.4	46.4	18.7	12.4	19.3
Chemicals	38.6	34.1	13.3	9.0	7.9	28.4	6.3	8.0	18.5	5.4
Manufactured exports	27.2	25.7	8.0	3.9	6.7	6.9	28.6	27.9	10.8	18.6

Source: United Nations/*ASEAN Economic Bulletin*

manufactures. But on the other hand, of course, electronics and electrical machinery have stepped in to give some compensation.

In the light of the sharpening trade tensions with both of its major trade partners, ASEAN is working on other markets, such as China and the EEC. There are hefty political obstacles to be overcome, however; for example, Beijing disapproves of Malaysia's racial policies. In the EEC, Portugal rejects Indonesia's annexation of

TABLE 8.6 ASEAN INTERNAL TRADE, AS A PROPORTION OF TOTAL ASEAN TRADE

	1975	1978	1980	1981	1982	1983
Intra-ASEAN trade (as % of ASEAN world trade)	14.7	15.6	17.3	17.3	21.1	22.5
ASEAN						
Exports	16.9	16.3	17.7	18.4	22.8	23.9
Imports	12.8	14.9	16.9	16.2	19.6	21.2
Indonesia*						
Exports	10.3	12.7	12.6	11.9	8.9	9.2
Imports	8.7	9.6	12.4	12.8	8.4	10.4
Malaysia						
Exports	24.2	18.5	22.4	26.6	30.0	28.8
Imports	15.2	14.3	16.4	17.9	19.9	19.7
Philippines						
Exports	2.7	6.2	6.5	7.2	7.1	7.1
Imports	4.8	5.6	6.2	6.6	6.5	8.6
Singapore*						
Exports	26.0	22.3	24.0	25.1	31.4	33.3
Imports	20.9	24.1	24.8	21.8	25.0	26.0
Thailand						
Exports	17.2	15.4	16.2	14.6	15.5	14.3
Imports	2.7	5.9	9.6	10.1	12.0	14.2

Source: IMF/*ASEAN Economic Bulletin*
Note: *Singapore does not publish figures for its trade with Indonesia. Statistics given are estimates based on Indonesian data.

East Timor and is proving a hindrance in European negotiations. Elsewhere, ASEAN's support for the exiled Pol Pot regime in Kampuchea continues to arouse controversy in much of Indochina.

But perhaps the most significant development of the last decade has been the increase in mutual trade between ASEAN's members. In 1983 22.5% of its world trade was internal, compared with only 14.7% in 1975. It would appeär that Singapore and the Philippines must be the mainspring of all this growth; but note also the increase in Thailand's local purchases (up from 2.7 to 14.2% of the regional total), as the country's normally close relationship with the USA has stumbled.

ASEAN itself is unhappy at the way its trade bodies are functioning. Opening the February 1985 conference in Kuala Lumpur, the Malaysian Premier Mahathir Mohamad said its achievements in the field of economic and trade promotion had been 'mediocre or worse'; he particularly bemoaned the lack of viable economic data, which he said had the potential to create an effective and co-ordinated economic system in the region.

VII The currency factor

Generally speaking, currency fluctuations have consistently worked in favour of the Pacific Basin. When the dollar is strong, exports are easy; when the yen is strong, it becomes easier to compete against Japan in the international markets. Nonetheless, there have been marked differences between those countries which have attempted to keep their currencies roughly aligned to the US dollar (Taiwan, Malaysia, Hong Kong and Singapore) and those which have abandoned this limitation in favour of the local market (South Korea, Indonesia and Thailand). With the rise in US protectionism and the increasing temptation to seek local markets it seems reasonable to expect that more of the NICs will adopt pricing systems which do not depend on developments in Washington.

South Korea, which decoupled the won from the US dollar in February 1980, has benefited since then from an effective devaluation of nearly 80%, and as the Japanese yen rose steeply in 1986 it was also able to step into that country's role as an exporter not only in the USA but in Europe, Canada and Australia. As has been outlined in Chapter Seven, its shipbuilding industry has been a particular beneficiary of the strong yen.

The Singapore dollar is managed by the authorities for parity against an undisclosed basket of foreign currencies; in practice, however, it has tended to stay closely aligned to the US currency. But the strength of the US dollar has proved a major setback in the mid-1980s, and both manufacturing costs and export prices have moved well ahead of the norm for the region as a whole. In 1985 the value of Singapore's exports fell by 2.3%, compounding the problems already pressing in the domestic economy, and it was only the subsequent decline of the US unit in 1986 which restored any growth to the country's trading performance.

Indonesia's currency, the rupiah, has been managed since November 1978 against a trade-weighted basket of foreign currencies, and the exchange rate has been allowed to fall considerably since then so as to maximise the country's export potential. In 1983 it was abruptly devalued by 27.5%, coinciding with the sharpening of conditions in the world petroleum market and a concerted effort to spread the range of its exports across the widest possible range. Apart from boosting sales the sliding rupiah has discouraged imports, which fell by 15% in 1984—a particularly timely development in view of the country's current problems, but still not enough to halt the decline into austerity.

Malaysia has historically done its best to manage its exchange rates for maximum stability against the US dollar. But this has proved a highly risky strategy in view of its considerable dependence on commodities, and since 1985 the government has had no choice but to let the currency weaken slowly against the US unit. By January 1987 the dollar rate had slid to 2.567 ringgits, about 10% down on the 2.32 ringgits average for 1983. Even so, Malaysia's exports are thought to be suffering from the continued strength of the currency.

Taiwan, too, has traditionally tried to keep its currency in line with the US unit—reflecting the fact that 48% of its exports went to the United States in 1985. The official dollar exchange rate in that year, at NT$ 39.85, was hardly changed from the NT$ 39.12 of three years earlier. As the year progressed, however, Taiwan found that its overvalued currency was depressing buying interest in the immediate Pacific region, and meanwhile there was growing import resistance in the all-important United States market, which had raised a number of specific trade grievances against Taipei. By January 1987 the rate had slid to NT$ 35.35, and was still falling despite the decline in the dollar itself. This is essential if Taiwan is to increase its trade with its partners in the Pacific Basin.

In the Philippines, the exchange rate was badly hit by the 1983 crisis of confidence which followed the killing of Benigno Aquino, and which precipitated a retraction of foreign investment, a freezing of foreign-currency bank accounts and the suspension of most foreign-currency dealings. Two devaluations in 1983 were followed by a third in June 1984, and by January 1987 the dollar rate, at 20.45 pesos, was 140% down on the 8.54 pesos being offered in 1982.

But paradoxically, the shift in the currency has done nothing very convincing for the country's export performance. In 1985 the volume of foreign sales fell by 2.5% even in peso terms—which meant a 13% decline when measured in dollars. Not even the restoration of party democracy in 1986 under a civilian president has done much to improve matters.

TABLE 8.7   PRINCIPAL TRADE PARTNERS, 1983/85

quarterly averages, in millions of US dollars

	Imports			Exports		
			2nd quarter			2nd quarter
	1983	1984	1985	1983	1984	1985
Hong Kong						
Total	6,002.4	7,141.8	7,557.0	5,490.7	7,079.4	7,536.0
Indonesia	32.5	38.2	32.7	149.6	131.9	105.9
South Korea	172.4	233.0	318.4	94.9	123.1	91.7
Malaysia	46.4	76.6	44.8	53.9	67.3	54.8
Philippines	40.8	60.3	49.4	94.6	82.6	68.5
Singapore	358.4	390.9	359.4	231.5	228.2	206.1
Thailand	81.0	70.3	72.1	60.5	61.5	52.6
China	1,461.4	1,782.7	1,745.1	623.8	1,270.2	2,164.8

TABLE 8.7   PRINCIPAL TRADE PARTNERS, 1983/85 *(continued)*

quarterly averages, in millions of US dollars

	Imports			Exports		
			2nd quarter			2nd quarter
	1983	**1984**	**1985**	**1983**	**1984**	**1985**
Japan	1,379.4	1,682.3	1,824.6	241.6	312.8	297.6
Australia	94.4	107.1	107.9	131.3	167.7	130.5
USA	657.6	779.4	761.5	1,765.9	2,349.2	2,254.1
Western Europe	848.0	1,073.7	1,001.2	1,052.4	1,205.8	1,018.1
Iran	0.1	—	0.1	5.1	3.9	2.8
Indonesia						
Total	4,087.8	3,470.0	—	5,286.5	5,470.2	—
Hong Kong	16.2	21.5	—	45.5	65.2	—
South Korea	97.0	53.5	—	81.8	148.8	—
Malaysia	15.0	21.5	—	14.5	24.5	—
Philippines	45.5	3.8	—	60.5	41.5	
Singapore	866.2	447.8	—	782.0	531.5	
Thailand	52.2	13.8	—	12.2	24.5	—
China	51.0	56.0	—	6.8	2.0	—
Japan	948.3	827.0	—	2,419.5	2,712.0	
Australia	100.5	93.0	—	52.0	68.8	—
USA	633.5	640.0	—	1,066.8	1,126.2	—
Western Europe	705.0	617.0	—	255.2	289.0	—
Iran	0.2	—	—	0.2	0.2	—
Japan						
Total	31,552	34,120	31,410	36,656	42,470	44,188
Hong Kong	167	210	221	1,319	1,637	1,502
Indonesia	2,603	2,792	2,490	886	767	503
South Korea	840	1,053	1,042	1,498	1,804	1,654
Malaysia	787	1,104	1,074	698	718	527
Philippines	326	354	302	435	270	258
Singapore	366	444	384	1,110	1,151	1,113
Thailand	254	260	263	626	605	464
China	1,272	1,490	1,626	1,228	1,802	3,258
Australia	1,658	1,824	1,950	1,068	1,295	1,396
USA	6,153	6,716	6,647	10,688	14,964	16,764

TABLE 8.7   PRINCIPAL TRADE PARTNERS, 1983/85 *(continued)*

quarterly averages, in millions of US dollars

	Imports		2nd quarter	Exports		2nd quarter
	1983	**1984**	**1985**	**1983**	**1984**	**1985**
Western Europe	2,769	3,271	3,137	5,678	5,992	6,394
Iran	1,057	717	395	703	422	378
South Korea						
Total	6,548.0	7,657.9	7,668.0	6,111.2	7,311.2	7,522.9
Hong Kong	55.3	117.0	81.7	204.4	320.3	360.4
Indonesia	96.8	163.2	132.2	63.1	63.5	59.3
Malaysia	194.3	251.3	252.9	56.7	63.3	67.5
Philippines	44.5	28.5	29.6	45.4	41.3	52.3
Singapore	100.2	97.6	55.9	134.7	124.2	95.3
Thailand	23.9	33.2	22.0	54.5	58.9	46.9
China	72.2	84.8	86.0	37.5	64.7	44.4
Japan	1,559.6	1,910.0	1,966.0	850.9	1,150.5	1,071.4
Australia	242.7	273.9	265.2	83.2	98.1	118.9
USA	1,568.6	1,718.9	1,755.9	2,061.4	2,619.7	2,894.2
Western Europe	684.9	883.6	949.2	950.8	1,012.0	1,139.1
Iran	—	—	—	—	—	—
Malaysia						
Total	3,310.2	3,514.2	—	3,531.9	4,140.8	—
Hong Kong	48.7	69.4	—	61.2	58.7	—
Indonesia	24.3	43.1	—	14.7	25:2	—
South Korea	59.7	63.0	—	165.3	207.2	—
Philippines	39.7	60.4	—	40.8	90.8	—
Singapore	461.1	459.7	—	795.5	845.1	—
Thailand	99.4	120.4	—	144.6	116.2	—
China	67.4	71.3	—	39.2	41.2	—
Japan	840.4	922.9	—	695.6	942.4	—
Australia	135.4	141.4	—	49.8	64.0	—
USA	531.8	573.8	—	465.9	557.7	—
Western Europe	545.9	563.6	—	563.7	577.4	—
Iran	24.1	—	—	15.4	8.0	—

154

TABLE 8.7   PRINCIPAL TRADE PARTNERS, 1983/85 *(continued)*

quarterly averages, in millions of US dollars

	Imports		2nd quarter	Exports		2nd quarter
	1983	1984	1985	1983	1984	1985
Papua New Guinea						
Total	243.6	237.2	—	205.6	218.4	—
Hong Kong	4.9	6.8	—	1.1	0.2	—
Indonesia	0.4	0.1	—	—	—	—
South Korea	1.1	1.0	—	9.4	15.5	—
Malaysia	0.9	0.9	—	0.7	—	—
Philippines	1.0	1.0	—	1.2	0.3	—
Singapore	32.7	30.0	—	3.8	4.1	—
Thailand	0.6	0.4	—	—	—	—
China	3.9	1.4	—	8.7	3.3	—
Japan	37.5	35.5	—	70.6	64.4	—
Australia	96.4	115.4	—	18.5	19.3	—
USA	24.2	13.2	—	4.6	7.6	—
Western Europe	20.0	12.1	—	79.8	96.1	—
Iran	—	—	—	—	—	—
Philippines						
Total	1,965.8	1,565.5	1,477.5	1,233.0	1,335.6	1,172.7
Hong Kong	66.2	60.6	50.9	39.6	58.6	41.0
Indonesia	44.2	49.8	71.6	7.6	2.0	5.7
South Korea	40.4	38.8	58.6	37.2	24.7	20.6
Malaysia	39.8	88.7	107.0	40.6	44.5	41.6
Singapore	72.4	29.9	30.0	34.8	80.3	69.8
Thailand	12.6	10.5	15.6	5.0	2.2	12.5
China	19.9	57.0	116.6	5.6	15.1	33.4
Japan	335.6	212.7	195.7	245.1	258.6	238.9
Australia	49.7	37.2	39.6	19.0	22.3	17.2
USA	457.8	428.4	346.0	448.2	507.9	398.4
Western Europe	265.6	196.5	112.6	237.6	223.7	198.5
Iran	8.9	—	17.9*	—	—	—
Singapore						
Total	7,039.6	7,177.9	6,591.7	5,458.1	6,026.9	5,822.0

TABLE 8.7   PRINCIPAL TRADE PARTNERS, 1983/85 *(continued)*

quarterly averages, in millions of US dollars

	Imports			Exports		
			2nd quarter			2nd quarter
	1983	1984	1985	1983	1984	1985
Hong Kong	150.0	150.4	124.2	370.4	372.6	383.8
Indonesia	—	—	—	—	—	—
South Korea	107.0	92.1	88.7	114.2	95.7	73.2
Malaysia	1,022.1	1,077.1	977.8	960.8	977.0	891.8
Philippines	32.1	46.4	40.8	105.1	51.9	57.0
Thailand	126.4	158.6	136.4	236.1	288.9	220.6
China	206.8	337.3	556.8	53.2	60.9	73.2
Japan	1,268.5	1,317.1	1,122.9	502.0	564.6	502.5
Australia	132.7	176.8	177.2	160.5	205.3	177.1
USA	1,071.4	1,046.6	1,003.4	988.7	1,207.5	1,250.6
Western Europe	856.5	876.5	919.4	579.8	666.2	696.8
Iran	144.3	85.9	238.1	96.9	85.2	141.8
Thailand						
Total	2,572.0	2,599.8	2,664.4	1,592.2	1,853.2	1,792.1
Hong Kong	29.2	32.2	31.2	79.2	70.4	72.1
Indonesia	8.4	19.9	21.6	29.9	11.7	13.5
South Korea	60.9	71.0	52.2	22.8	30.6	20.5
Malaysia	138.4	126.2	177.0	71.3	87.7	101.7
Philippines	3.9	5.0	9.6	16.9	5.7	20.2
Singapore	159.0	206.6	172.3	129.5	155.8	146.5
China	66.2	79.2	57.8	26.8	50.4	80.6
Japan	703.9	700.2	653.4	240.0	241.2	222.9
Australia	46.7	48.8	38.9	23.4	30.3	28.6
USA	322.9	347.5	301.7	238.0	318.0	346.5
Western Europe	409.3	396.6	524.9	375.2	419.6	364.2
Iran	—	—	—	25.8	31.1	9.6

Source:

Note: *1st quarter

VIII   Back-door exports: the unofficial side of Pacific trade

No survey of the Pacific Basin economies would be complete without at least mentioning in passing the very substantial amount of trade which goes unrecorded. In some of the developing countries (notably Thailand and Indonesia) it might account for a third of all exports; in other, more developed states (especially Taiwan and Singapore), its importance is acknowledged but its volume is still blacked out from the figures with official blessing. The object of the following, then, is not to try and quantify the extent of back-door trade, but to list some of the *caveats* which should be borne in mind when looking at trade statistics.

To start with the most well-known example: Singapore does not, as a matter of course, include Indonesia when publishing its official trade statistics. This is particularly inconvenient since, according to Indonesia, it sells over US$ 2,000 mn worth of products to or through Singapore—which would be equivalent to 7.6% of Singapore's total imports in 1985.

The results of this omission are apt to distort not only Singapore's own trade figures but those of the ASEAN group as a whole. In the past, Malaysia (the host country to the organisation) has generally been the most reliable source of data.

Occasionally, references to specific transactions are discouraged for political and foreign policy reasons. Taiwan does not publicise its rapidly growing dealings with the People's Republic of China— which it still regards officially as its own territory. Consequently the detailed statistics issued by the Council for Economic Planning and Development in Taipei are quite badly flawed. Taiwan, not being a member of the United Nations, is generally omitted from UN and International Monetary Fund statistics; satisfactory figures are often available from US sources, however.

Different countries adopt varying methods of accounting for the freeport activity on which an increasing number are pinning their future hopes. It is often advisable to confirm whether export figures include the re-export of unprocessed goods (as is sometimes the case in Hong Kong).

As in all developing countries, countertrade is on the increase and probably represents the largest single off-the-record factor in the region at present. By securing one commodity directly against another, it offers protection against fluctuating world prices and varying exchange rates, and this is particularly attractive to commodity producers such as Malaysia—one of the region's more active countertraders. Often the deals involve three or more countries in what are known as switch-trading operations, and their popularity is evident from the fact that several of the major international banks have now opened special divisions for the preparation of such deals.

Ironically, there is something of a shortage of countertrade expertise in Hong Kong, the trading centre best placed to tackle the burgeoning barter and switch-trade market in China. Beijing has made no secret of its desire to develop this side of its trading activities, and has shown itself to be a shrewd negotiator. US calculations indicate that China's barter deals totalled $6,000 mn in 1985—of which $2,000 mn was with the Soviet Union.

Finally, a few words should be added about the illegal side of Pacific business: smuggling, drugs and counterfeit goods. It is widely believed that drugs and other black-market goods produce up to half of Thailand's foreign exchange, much of the resulting contraband passing overland through Burma. In Malaysia and Indonesia strong measures are being undertaken to stop this kind of trade, but it remains highly profitable for the operators and may still contribute up to a fifth of true export revenues.

It is in Taiwan, however, where the most sophisticated market in counterfeit goods is to be found. The expertise of small forgers extends well beyond such traditional items as perfumes, cigarettes and audio and video tapes; nowadays whole microcomputers are being faked and sold, presumably with some degree of official acquiescence, on the international black market. Little of it, presumably, is being officially recorded in the trade figures.

The United States has shown itself very concerned over this switch toward high-technology, low-turnover forgeries, and it has been threatening severe trade reprisals unless it receives government assurances that Taiwan's booming counterfeit business will be reined in. Pressure is also mounting on South Korea, where the copying of high-technology goods for export has gone well beyond the limits of mere patent infringement.

As the Pacific region gears up to extend its international business beyond its traditional trading partners, Japan and the USA, it is likely that the incentives will grow to clamp down on all forms of illegal trade; but with the spread of cheap high-technology manufacturing equipment and the improvement in world communications markets (not to mention the profusion of secretive offshore banking centres in the Pacific region), the potential for such unofficial trading activities is if anything increasing.

Chapter Nine

THE FUTURE OF THE PACIFIC BASIN: PROBLEMS AND OPPORTUNITIES

I Overall outlook

To what degree can the dynamic countries of the Pacific Basin, the NICs in particular, sustain their extraordinary recent economic performance? This question is of considerable importance to the NICs' trade partners, foreign investors and economic policy managers. There are some reasons for believing that their outstanding growth record can persist, and some factors which point to difficulties in the short and medium term.

To take the positive factors first, the growth of the countries' factors of production is essentially favourable on all counts. The skills of their labour forces are being increased. Literacy is virtually universal, and secondary and tertiary educational enrolments are growing, while technical and managerial skills have been building up in parallel with industrial capacity. The ethnic composition of many of the countries, particularly with their Chinese component, tends also to favour entrepreneurship.

As for their physical capital stock, the infrastructure or social capital of most countries is continually under improvement. Seoul, for instance, for a country at its stage of development enjoys excellent subway, surface transport, road, telephone, sewerage and power facilities. Plant and equipment have been built up at dramatic rates over the past 10 to 15 years, and the evidence from measures of productivity, such as the incremental capital-output ratio, is that this plant is being used increasingly efficiently over time. The high rates of capital utilisation common throughout the region attest to the appropriateness of past investment decisions while also helping the overall efficiency of the industrial sector.

As well as the factors of production growing in abundance, the planning procedures with which the governments of the region try to orchestrate policy show signs of liberalisation and improvements. The general drift of policy—as commented upon elsewhere in this book—is towards diminishing the power of the state in economic decision-making.

The factors which are likely, on the other hand, to inhibit continued economic growth among the NICs can be grouped into external and internal. Chief among the external factors is the simple fact that governments in many of their trading partners are prey to protectionist pressures of various strengths and types. This single fact will probably do more to colour the economic prospects of the NICs than any other in the next ten to fifteen years. Exports, as discussed earlier, have been the major engine of growth throughout the NICs' high period. Further constraints to this export growth will thus necessarily have a severe impact on overall growth-rates, through the channels of lower foreign exchange earnings, lower corporate profitability, slower growth of employment and tax revenues, and more difficult debt servicing. This problem will remain severe in the European export markets, since, of the major developed country markets, Europe is that in which low economic growth and unemployment problems will be most severe. In the US, protectionism may continue its erratic and confused path so long as unemployment remains tolerably low and the dollar's fall from its 1984–85 peaks erodes the cost-competitiveness of imports. In Japan, demand for goods from the NICs is to a large degree derived demand, reflecting in part demand for Japanese products in Japan's own export markets. To the extent that Europe and the US remain difficult markets for Japanese exporters, exporters in the NICs will feel some of the difficulty too. A variety of expedient 'solutions' to protectionism is likely to be tried by companies based in the NICs; they will include direct investment inside their main markets (e.g. Hyundai with its North American auto plants); joint sourcing ventures (e.g. Yue Loong with Ford); and a virtually infinite variety of out-sourcing, local assembly and partial-processing ploys.

In general terms, the climate within which international trade takes place has become tighter over the past ten years. The Kennedy round of multilateral trade negotiations, which took place during 1964 to 1967, cut tariffs by 50% except on items designated as sensitive—such as textiles and footwear. At the subsequent GATT round, the so-called Tokyo Round of 1973–79, there were again sizeable cuts in nominal tariff rates, of between 26% and 59%, with sensitive items again exempt. Since that time, however, the

162

drift has very much been toward greater use of non-tariff barriers (NTBs) such as quotas (restricting to a certain volume the amount of imports a country will tolerate), voluntary export restraints (a misleadingly-termed variant on quotas) and restrictive standards. The impact of these NTBs over the last decade has been, cumulatively, to restrict the access—sometimes severely—of many developing country producers to markets in developed countries. Asian countries have been particularly affected insofar as the composition of their exports is moving towards manufactured and other processed goods, rather than raw materials or low value-added goods. Moreover, many of the 'sensitive' goods protected particularly carefully in developed countries are precisely those in which Pacific Basin manufacturers have shown strong comparative advantage.

The trade tensions increasingly associated with Asian exporters to the US (and the rest of the developed world) are particularly severe in the case of the Japanese trade surplus. Japan's surplus with the rest of the world grew to a record in the first half of the 1985/86 fiscal year. In the six months ending in September 1985, Japan's current account surplus grew to $26.6 bn (seasonally unadjusted), compared to $18.6 bn a year before. This figure largely reflected a massive visible trade surplus of $29.3 bn (up from $23.1 bn a year earlier). The main source of growth in that trade flow was a 7.2% rise in exports to the US. Total exports reached $86.7 bn, a 1.6% increase over the year, while imports totalled $57.4 bn, a 7.6% fall. Falling prices for oil and other raw materials lay behind that decline.

If Japan's exports have been continuing to grow, however, the Asian NICs have lately been finding it difficult to maintain their earlier rates of export growth. Export growth in Taiwan slowed down appreciably in 1985, and indeed in the first three quarters of 1985 exports fell slightly to $25.5 bn, compared to the previous year. Its current account should, however, continue to be substantially in surplus; the 1984 current account surplus of $7 bn could be repeated in 1985. South Korea's balance of payments deficit grew from $1.33 bn in the first seven months of 1984 to $1.63 bn in the same period in 1985, with falls in foreign orders of footwear, wooden goods, textiles and electronics responsible. Hong Kong's export composition is still heavily weighted by textiles and apparel, with 40% of merchandise exports being accounted for by such goods. This predominance has not fallen in five years. The exposure of these goods to protectionist moves by Japan as well as the US makes for a highly erratic export growth-path; between the first half of 1984 and 1985 exports to the US fell by 11%, to the UK by 18% and to Japan by 11%. In Singapore, too, export growth has contracted, and 1985 was expected to be the first year in decades when GNP did not grow at all.

Recent export performance of the Pacific Basin countries has tended to suffer due to a number of factors.

First, a number of their currencies (notably those of Hong Kong, Korea, Taiwan and Singapore) have been linked to the US dollar, and the precipitate rise of that currency has threatened the price exports from countries with related currencies out of their export markets. Secondly, as far as the product composition of the Pacific countries is concerned, the heavy weighting of electronic components and consumer goods has tended to act as a drag on their growth, as US imports of these items decelerated. Next, the OPEC countries, which became large importers of Pacific Basin goods (not to mention labour) after the mid 1970s, substantially cut their imports as oil prices declined and their export earnings contracted. Fourth, in certain product areas (consumer electronics are a case in point) substitution of capital for labour in developed countries is eroding the lower labour cost advantage the Pacific countries enjoyed earlier. In the case of certain electronics assembly processes, robots and other highly mechanised production systems are deployed by US plants which offset the loss of cheap assembly labour by eliminating trans-Pacific transportation costs while offering tighter delivery and inventory control. A final factor which, while small, now is likely to grow in importance over time, is the tendency for US protectionism to lead to Asian-owned plants to be built within the US. Examples include the auto assembly plant of Hyundai planned for Canada, and Lucky Gold Star's TV plant opened in the US in 1982. In cases such as these, visible export revenues are partially replaced by inflows of overseas earnings through the capital account.

On the positive side, the growth of imports by China is likely to continue to offer opportunities to Pacific Basin exporters. This is particularly important for the less diversified exporters such as

164

Taiwan, 49% of whose exports by value went to the US in 1984 (up from 36% in 1981).

II Prospects by country

Despite a general slowdown in export performance, Japan is far from being the only country with which the US has been running a large bilaterial trade deficit. Taiwan had a $2.09 bn trade surplus with the US in 1980; by 1984 this had grown to $9.8 bn. (The US accounts for 49% of total Taiwanese exports; the second most important trading partner is Japan, which absorbed 10% of Taiwan's exports in 1984.) Political pressures in the US have arisen over Taiwan's having high tariffs on many imports, such as cigarettes, wine and beer, where the US might reasonably hope to compete successfully. A total of 192 tariff items were relaxed in late 1985, with 20% tariff cuts enacted. Partly in return, the US Trade Representative agreed not to pursue unfair trade practices investigations.

Although it has been running a sizeable overall trade deficit, Korea has also been under pressure to liberalise its trade policy. In October 1985 the Korean Government announced a plan to relax import restrictions on hundreds of manufactured goods, although this was hedged with a plan to levy tariffs on many of the goods just released from quota protection.

The small Asian economies have been exerting pressure on the Japanese Government to help relieve the trade tensions arising with the US, since the small economies' successes, while modest in terms of total world trade, tend to be lumped together with the Japanese 'trade threat' by US politicians.

Among the internal constraints on continued high growth, political instability ranks as among the most serious. Hong Kong is scheduled to revert to Chinese ownership in 1997; how this will affect the behaviour of its economy is hard to tell. Initial fears once the British had agreed on the outlines of a settlement with the Chinese in 1984 came to be reconsidered in 1985, with the stock market and the once-depressed real estate market recovering substantially. In Singapore, the main questions concern the succession to Lee Kuan Yew, while there is a similar succession problem arising in Taiwan. In Korea there is steady pressure from students and other disaffected groups on the government and in the Philippines the new Aquino administration has yet to prove that it can control the country in the aftermath of the oppressive Marcos regime.

Labour shortage is a potential brake on the development of Singapore and Taiwan. As demand for labour continues to grow during periods of full employment, wage inflation is bound to ensue. Given the labour-intensive nature of much of the NICs' exports— even from the highest-income countries like Singapore—this is bound to create problems of transition. In anticipation of this problem, the Singapore Government tried with its 1979 National Wages Council policy to hasten the economy's shift out of lower value-added items and into skill-intensive activities like developing computer software, but the policy was not an unqualified success. In 1985, wages in Singapore were due to grow by between 3% and 7%, after negotiations between the government-monitored National Wage Council and the employers. Trade union membership has been falling in Singapore, down from about 250,000 in 1979 to 192,000 in 1984. In Taiwan severe skill shortages are likely to emergy by 1990. The Council for Economic Planning and Development has suggested that demand for labour will grow by an average of 2.2% per year between 1985 and 1993. Although this marks a deceleration from the 3.5% per year rate seen in the 1975–85 period, it is high enough to push Taiwan up the Asian wages league table. In 1984, Taiwanese manufacturing wages outstripped those of South Korea for the first time, with an 18% rise in average earnings to $325 per month in Taiwan as against a 4.1% rise to $304 per month in South Korea.

In South Korea wages have tended to lag behind in terms of overall economic growth in recent years. A survey in 1985 found that roughly half of all workers in firms employing five or more people earn less than $230 per month. Partly as a result, labour unrest has been growing, with more strikes, and longer strikes. In 1984 there were 113 strikes recorded. Some reform of the country's vigorously anti-union labour legislation has been expected for a while, but with the climate of tougher export markets being experienced in 1985 such reform is likely to be postponed.

An important aspect of the Pacific Basin governments' economic thinking is the increasing awareness they are exhibiting of being in competition with their neighbours for private foreign investment projects. South Korea and Taiwan in particular appear to be highly aware of one another's actions. Both countries' governments are moving steadily down a path of liberalisation—letting foreigners invest in a wider range of industries, letting them take a bigger equity share of each project, letting them repatriate profits more easily, and giving them faster project approval. In Taiwan foreign inflows totalled $559 mn in 174 projects; cumulative investments by foreigners grew to $4.46 bn in 3,297 projects.

Taiwan has consistently enjoyed larger foreign capital inflows than has South Korea, due in large part to its more relaxed investment policies. Both governments are aware of factors which could, however, threaten this continued growth, such as the fact that China is a natural location for labour-intensive manufacturing and assembly operations, and both South Korea and Taiwan, with per capita incomes by 1990 expected to be in the $2,900–$4,000 range, will be unable to compete directly. Moreover, the Indonesian Government, anxious to diversify exports now that oil revenues are declining, is also emphasising labour-intensive industries.

Another potential problem for the Pacific Basin economies is the fact that their banking and other financial institutions have tended not to grow in sophistication at the same pace as their industries. Thus, at the mid-1980s many countries are saddled with banking systems which have lent on overly generous terms to a small number of officially-favoured borrowers, tend to discriminate against small business lending, tend to have serious problems with as yet unrecognised bad loans, and tend to suffer from fraud and abuse on a large scale. Taken together these problems may act to constrain the economies' ability to finance the restructuring needed to compete effectively in the world economy.

South Korea provides many examples of these problems. The banks were used by the government for much of the industrial reconstruction period as merely the official channelling agent for lending decisions already made by ministers and other non-bank officials. This has had two effects. First, the banking system now has a very lopsided portfolio of loans, with the big 30 corporate groups, the *chaebol*, accounting for much of the lending. The bad loans generated within these groups were estimated in mid-1985 to be $4.6 bn. The big construction groups alone are owed in the order of $2 bn by clients in the Middle East, for whom they worked on projects such as refineries and petrochemical complexes. Exacerbating these problems is the high leverage of the *chaebol;* debt/equity ratios average 5:1. The second effect of this use of the banks is that few experienced lending officers have grown up in the system. Thus, should the banks embrace wholeheartedly the new orthodoxy of loan diversification and entrepreneurial lending, they would be prone to making a second round of bad decisions.

In an effort to invigorate the country's capital markets, the government is liberalising conditions for foreign banks. The 52 foreign bank branches should, for instance, enjoy similar rights as domestic banks, following legislative changes proposed in 1984. US banks in particular have been pushing for this type of change. The government of South Korea has, in addition, taken the step of injecting a large amount of liquidity into the system to stabilise the banks while they try to clean up their balance sheets. Finally, the authorities would also like to bring the illegal so-called 'kerb market', whereby borrowers not lucky enough to be on the old approved list went underground for loans, into mainstream banking.

In late 1985 the South Korean Government took a further step towards diversifying companies' funding sources by allowing them to issue convertible bonds and depositary receipts overseas. The Ministry of Finance thus allowed foreigners to invest directly in South Korean companies; hitherto, such investment had to be via trust funds. At first only 14 companies out of the 340 listed on the stock exchange are to issue such bonds, on the grounds that only those with net assets in excess of 50 bn won (about $56 mn) are suitable for foreign participation. Samsung Electronics Co. was one of the first to take advantage of this opportunity with a $20 mn bond issue announced in November 1985. Even for Samsung, however, the convertibility of the bonds created a problem in that the price of the stock into which the bond would ultimately be converted was so volatile in 1985 that investors could not be sure how to value the bond.

Taiwan has seen similar problems. A large underground loan market has developed there in response to banks' reluctance to lend much to companies, which by convention reveal very little verifiable financial data about themselves. In the Cathay debacle of 1985, for instance, a lot of borrowing had been undertaken merely to service the interest charges—of up to 30% per year—being levied on the old loans. Although the government still owns or controls all the banks in the country, and calls have been made for substantial liberalisation, not least by senior officials in the three large state-owned commercial banks, by end-1985 there were few signs of major reform underway. In the stockmarket, by contrast, efforts to open up stock ownership to foreigners, through the agency of three investment funds, reflect a desire to broaden the range of financial instruments with which companies can fuel their growth. Short-term bank loans from the kerb market are recognised as being sub-optional from a national or social, as well as private, point of view, and it is hoped that a deeper stock market will allow companies to grow with less awesome leverage.

Malaysia's banking system is more sophisticated, in that there is strong competition on lending rates among different institutions, including merchant banks and finance companies. Nonetheless, problems of over-zealous lending against shaky collateral, such as for property building and securities purchases, have resulted in some major upsets. The official preferences given to native Malays (or bumiputras) has also caused problems. Banks' liquidity ratios have never been under threat in recent years due to lower corporate earnings.

In the Philippines the story is similar again. In mid-1985 the country's eighteenth-largest bank, the Pacific Banking Corp., went bankrupt, as a result of bad loans, notably in real estate. The authorities had spent some $100 mn in rescue efforts until then. Reform of the whole banking system, to facilitate lending to farmers and small businesses, and possibility to consolidate the various government-owned banks, is being contemplated.

As in other countries, the Philippine stock market is thinly traded and subject to upsets which can undermine the fabric of its professionalism and the trust that investors place in it. In 1985 the stock market suffered from the government's extraordinary efforts at reducing the country's prevailing rate of inflation, then 60% per year. In an effort to absorb excessive money supply in the economy, the central bank issued bonds with very high yields—for a while, in excess of 45%. When investors, quite rationally, switched out of stocks and into bonds to take advantage of this return, the stock market suffered a collapse in trading, and a number of brokers went out of business.

Difficulties can also be expected to arise in some of the Pacific Basin economies because of the tendency for a handful of large companies to dominate each economy. These big conglomerates, which have arisen in some cases through official favouritism and in other cases through networks of family-controlled mergers, may yield sub-optimal investment decisions for the economy as a whole and may tend to grow through excessive leverage, creating acute problems if some of their debts turn bad.

TABLE 9.1   TERMS OF PUBLIC BORROWING

	Commit- ments $ mn		Average interest rate (%)		Average maturity (years)		Average grace period (years)	
	1970	1983	1970	1983	1970	1983	1970	1983
Australia	—	—	—	—	—	—	—	—
Hong Kong	—	—	—	7.5	—	12	—	4
Indonesia	518	5,597	2.7	8.8	34	15	9	5
Japan	—	—	—	—	—	—	—	—
South Korea	677	3,320	6.0	9.8	19	12	5	4
Malaysia	83	3,101	6.1	9.5	19	11	5	6
New Zealand	—	—	—	—	—	—	—	—
Philippines	158	1,814	7.4	9.1	11	16	2	5
Singapore	69	82	6.8	9.7	17	9	4	2
Weighted average: upper middle- income countries	—	—	6.9	11.0	13	10	4	3

Source: World Bank

The Pacific Basin countries' indebtedness varies in nature and degree. For some countries, such as Malaysia, rapid growth of debt in recent years suggests that considerable domestic policy changes will be needed to ensure orderly management of the repayments in future. In other countries, such as Singapore, debt is relatively low and can be easily managed. Table 9.1 shows the basics of public borrowing in each country, and indicates how the average maturity of debt fell for all countries between 1970 and 1983 and how, reflecting international conditions, the later debt has been written at higher interest rates than the older commitments. Debt-service ratios, as shown in Table 9.2 are one way of showing a country's expected ease of repayments. One measure shows what proportion of foreign currency earnings from exports will have to be used to pay off the principle and interest of outstanding debts. In this case, for South Korea for instance, the debt-service ratio has actually fallen over the 1970–83 period, from 19.4% to 12.3%. These amounts are relatively modest by comparison with many other countries: in Argentina, for instance, 52% of estimated 1985 current account earnings will be absorbed by interest payments. The highest figure for Asia for 1985 is the Philippines, estimated at 28%, followed by South Korea and Indonesia at 12% each, then Malaysia at 9%.

TABLE 9.2 STRUCTURE OF EXTERNAL PUBLIC DEBT

	External debt outstanding				Debt service as % of:			
	$ mn		as % of GNP		GNP		Exports of goods and services	
	1970	1983	1970	1983	1970	1983	1970	1983
Australia	—	—	—	—	—	—	—	—
Hong Kong	2	224	0.1	0.8	—	0.2	—	—
Indonesia	2,443	21,685	27.1	28.9	0.9	3.4	6.9	12.8
Japan	—	—	—	—	—	—	—	—
South Korea	1,797	21,472	—	—	—	—	19.4	12.3
Malaysia	390	10,665	10.0	38.6	1.7	3.5	3.6	5.9
New Zealand	—	—	—	—	—	—	—	—
Philippines	572	10,385	8.1	30.4	1.4	3.7	7.2	15.4
Singapore	152	1,244	7.9	7.6	0.6	2.4	0.6	1.3
Average: upper middle-income countries	n/a	n/a	11.5	31.7	1.7	4.7	10.8	17.4

Source: World Bank

All the evidence from the Pacific Basin economies' national plans points to their governments' having highly ambitious plans. The sixth five-year plan of Korea, for 1987 to 1991, for instance, calls for growth of GNP from $81 bn in 1984 to $130 bn (in 1980 prices) by 1991. Fuelled by a 9% per year growth of export volumes, GNP per capita is scheduled to rise from its 1984 level of $1,994 to $2,910 by 1991. The Korea Development Institute's long-term planning for the year 2000 points to per capita income of $5,103 (stated in 1984 dollars), reflecting annual average growth of GNP of 6.2% in 1985–1990 and 6.0% in 1991–2000.

The very impressive rates of economic growth, and export growth, recorded by the most dynamic members of the Pacific Basin

TABLE 9.3   MANUFACTURED EXPORTS TO THE USA[1]

1984	Total US$ billion	As % total exports to world	As % of GNP	As % of total US manufactured imports
W. Europe	50.3	7	2	23
Japan	57.9	34	12	27
Canada	41.6	47	13	19
Taiwan	15.3	50	28	7
South Korea	9.7	33	12	5
Hong Kong	8.7	31	28	4
Mexico	7.1	29	10	3
Brazil	3.9	15	2	2
Singapore	3.6	15	24	2
Philippines	1.8	34	8	1
India	1.4	14	1	1
Malaysia	2.2	13	9	1
Indonesia	0.6	10	7	1
China	2.2	9	1	1
Chile	0.3	9	5	1
12 LDCs	56.8	23	5	26
World Total	217.0	—	—	100

Sources: US Department of Commerce, IMF

Note: [1]Includes machinery and transport equipment

economy has however led to a general overstating of their importance in the world economy. While they may account for a significant portion of world output of a few narrow products— certain types of footwear, for instance—they remain to a large extent peripheral to the world economy. For instance, South Korea's share of world export value in 1984, despite its record $26.3 bn export performance, was a mere 1.5%. Table 9.3 shows, for 1984, the share of the Pacific Basin economies' manufactures exports in total US imports of manufactures. It can be seen, despite decades of explosive export growth, that each of these countries remains peripheral to world trade flows. Indeed, it is only when aggregated that the importance of these countries as exporters to the US begins to approach that of Japan, with a 26% aggregate share of US manufactures imports against 27% for Japan.

Summing up, it would appear that the economy of the Pacific Basin has a great deal of potential. The factor inputs needed to sustain high rates of economic growth are, for the most part, there. When seen in the light of the economic policy stance usually taken in these countries, which is to let the market equilibrate shortages and surpluses, there is probably little reason to fear chronic resource allocation problems in the years ahead. Most of the threats to these countries' prospects are, by contrast, external; chief among them is the trade policy stance of the developed countries. How well these difficulties can be managed, and whether the expected new round of GATT international trade talks will help, remains to be seen.

Chapter Ten
STATISTICAL DATAFILE

TABLE 10.1   POPULATION DISTRIBUTION

	Population ('000)	Area ('000 sq km)	Persons per sq km	% urban
Australia	16,200	7,682	2	64
Hong Kong	5,466	0.4	5,119	92
Indonesia	165,153	1,905	87	24
Japan	121,050	378	320	76
South Korea	42,400	99	429	62
Malaysia	15,190	329	46	31
New Zealand	3,100	269	12	50
Philippines	54,350	301	181	39
Singapore	2,750	0.6	4,583	100

Source: IMF, National statistics

TABLE 10.2   TRENDS IN POPULATION SIZE

	1980	1982	1984	1986 estimates
Australia	14,700	15,180	15,540	16,200
Hong Kong	5,040	5,230	5,364	5,596
Indonesia	146,360	153,040	159,890	167,200
Japan	117,060	118,449	120,018	121,000
South Korea	38,120	39,330	40,580	42,400
Malaysia	13,760	14,400	15,190	15,700
New Zealand	3,100	3,160	3,230	3,280
Philippines	48,320	50,740	53,170	54,500
Singapore	2,414	2,472	2,529	2,570

Source: IMF, UN, National statistics

TABLE 10.3   VITAL STATISTICS, 1983

	Births (per '000)	Deaths (per '000)	Male life expectancy (years)	Female life expectancy (years)	Adult literacy (%)
Australia	15.5*	7.1	72	79	82
Hong Kong*	14.5	4.8*	73	78	90
Indonesia	30.7	13.0	51	54	36
Japan	12.6	6.2	74	80	95
South Korea*	23.0	6.2	63	69	93
Malaysia	29.2	5.8	67	72	60
New Zealand	25.8	8.1	71	77	84
Philippines	32.3	6.9	63	66	83
Singapore	16.2	5.3	69	74	85

Source: United Nations, Estimates
Notes: *1984

TABLE 10.4   POPULATION BREAKDOWN BY SEX

	Year	Total ('000)	Male %	Female %
Australia	1981	14,576	49.9	50.1
Hong Kong	1981	4,987	52.2	47.8
Indonesia	1980	146,776	49.7	50.3
Japan	1980	117,060	49.2	50.8
South Korea	1980	37,436	50.1	49.9
Malaysia	1980	13,436	50.2	49.8
New Zealand	1981	3,176	49.7	50.3
Philippines	1980	48,098	50.2	49.8
Singapore	1985	2,558	50.9	49.1

Source: United Nations

176

TABLE 10.5   EMPLOYMENT/UNEMPLOYMENT

	Year	Labour force ('000s)	% of population	Unemployed ('000s) latest year	% of labour force
Australia	1985	7,400	45.7	629	8.5
Hong Kong	1985	2,879	48.8	98	3.4
Indonesia	1983	59,599	37.4	6,000	10.0
Japan	1985	60,000*	49.5	1,560	2.6
South Korea	1984	14,984	36.9	465	3.1
Malaysia	1985	5,576	36.7	390	7.0
New Zealand	1986	1,400	45.2	53	3.8
Philippines	1983	19,212	35.3	1,191	6.2
Singapore	1984	1,175	45.9	39	3.3

Source: National statistics
Note: *Estimates

TABLE 10.6   EMPLOYMENT BY SECTOR

% breakdown

	Year	Labour force ('000s)	Agriculture	Services	Industry & construction
Australia	1985	7,400	6.0	72.5	21.5
Hong Kong	1985	2,879	2.0	60.4	30.5
Indonesia	1986	54,000*	48.0	30.0*	10.0*
Japan	1985	60,000*	8.5	69.3	22.2
South Korea	1984	14,984	26.0	48.0	23.0
Malaysia	1985	5,576	35.5	41.9	22.6
New Zealand	1983/84	1,400	10.9	65.8	23.3
Philippines	1983	19,212	51.4	34.6	14.0
Singapore	1984	1,175	7.5	56.4	36.1

Source: National statistics
Note: *Estimates

TABLE 10.7   GROSS DOMESTIC PRODUCT

	Currency (millions)	1983	1984	1985	GDP per capita, latest year units	GDP $ mn
Australia	Aus. dollar	175,640	200,600	222,570	13,739	148,380
Hong Kong	HK dollar	183,315	232,700	234,560	43,253	30,072
Indonesia	Rupiah (bns)	73,698	85,914	—	537,000	79,994
Japan	Yen (bns)	280,257	298,084	317,616	2,624,923	1,332,000
South Korea	Won (bns)	59,603	67,126	—	1,654,000	81,168
Malaysia	Ringgit	69,910	79,634	78,000	5,135	32,165
New Zealand	NZ dollar	34,935	40,978	41,185	12,000*	31,400
Philippines	Peso	384,690	549,670	623,100	11,458	32,740
Singapore	S dollar	35,171	38,733	36,800	15,244	15,930

Source: IMF, National statistics,
Note: *Estimate

TABLE 10.8   GDP BREAKDOWN, BY SECTOR

%

	Year	Agriculture	Services	Industry & construction
Australia	1985	5.7	58.0	36.3
Hong Kong	1984	0.5	69.7	29.8
Indonesia	1983/84	26.4	17.2	21.4
Japan	1983	5.2	56.5	38.3
South Korea	1984	14.7	55.2	30.1
Malaysia	1985	29.3	43.3	27.4
New Zealand	1983/84	9.1	62.1	28.8
Philippines	1984	26.2	49.1	24.7
Singapore	1984	0.8	73.2	26.0

Source: National statistics

TABLE 10.9   SECTORAL DEVELOPMENT, 1973–1983

Average annual growth rates, 1973–1983

	GDP	Agriculture	Manufacturing	Services
Australia	2.9	1.2	2.0	4.0
Hong Kong	9.3	1.1	−8.2	9.8
Indonesia	7.0	3.7	12.6	9.0
Japan	4.3	−1.6	−5.5	8.3
South Korea	7.3	1.5	11.8	6.8
Malaysia	7.3	4.4	−8.7	8.2
New Zealand	1.9	−1.0	−1.9	4.0
Philippines	5.4	4.3	5.0	5.2
Singapore	8.2	1.5	7.9	8.1

Source: World Bank, National statistics, Estimates

TABLE 10.10   INFLATION RATES

% per annum

	1982	1983	1984	1985
Australia	8.8	8.1	5.5	6.5
Hong Kong	10.5	9.9	8.1	3.2
Indonesia	9.5	12.4	10.4	4.7
Japan	2.7	1.7	2.3	4.0
South Korea	7.3	3.4	2.3	2.5
Malaysia	5.8	3.7	3.9	0.3
New Zealand	16.2	7.3	14.0	15.4
Philippines	10.1	10.0	5.0	—
Singapore	3.8	1.2	2.6	0.4

Source: IMF, National statistics

TABLE 10.11   EXCHANGE RATES, 1982–1986

Unit of currency per US dollar,
yearly averages at market rates

	1982	1983	1984	1985	June 1986
Australia	0.8	1.1	1.2	1.5	1.5
Hong Kong	5.1	7.8	7.8	7.8	7.8
Indonesia	626.8	994.0	1,074.0	1,125.0	1,131.0
Japan	203.0	232.2	251.1	200.5	165.0
South Korea	659.9	795.5	827.4	890.2	886.6
Malaysia	2.2	2.3	2.4	2.4	2.6
New Zealand	1.0	1.5	2.1	2.0	1.8
Philippines	7.5	11.1	16.7	18.7	20.5
Singapore	2.1	2.1	2.1	2.1	2.2

Source: IMF, National statistics

TABLE 10.12   INTEREST RATES

	Type	1980	1981	1982	1983	1984	1985
Australia	Money market	10.3	12.1	13.9	9.5	10.8	14.7
Hong Kong	Lending rate	—	16.5	10.5	13.5	11.0	7.0
Indonesia	Money market	12.9	16.3	17.2	13.2	18.6	10.3
Japan	Discount rate	7.3	5.5	5.5	5.0	5.0	5.0
South Korea	Discount rate	16.0	11.0	5.0	5.0	5.0	5.0
Malaysia	Discount rate	4.5	4.5	5.1	5.2	5.1	—
New Zealand	Discount rate	14.0	13.0	13.0	7.5	13.5	19.8
Philippines	Discount rate	11.0	—	—	—	—	—
Singapore	Money market	11.0	11.5	7.9	7.1	7.7	—

Source: IMF, National statistics

TABLE 10.13   TRENDS IN GROSS FIXED INVESTMENT

	Currency (millions)	1981	1982	1983	1984
Australia	Aus. dollar	38,690	41,940	41,240	45,180
Hong Kong	HK dollar	56,050	57,792	55,250	56,900
Indonesia	Rupiah (bns)	11,553	13,467	21,668	22,566
Japan	Yen (bns)	78,941	79,987	79,217	82,973
South Korea	Won (bns)	13,208	15,676	18,605	20,176
Malaysia	Ringgit	20,365	23,457	25,363	26,658
New Zealand	NZ dollar	6,215	7,436	7,928	8,820
Philippines	Peso	79,290	86,030	95,250	105,590
Singapore	S dollar	11,988	14,795	16,623	—

Source: IMF, National statistics

TABLE 10.14   PRIVATE SECTOR CONSUMPTION

	Currency	Year	Total consumption	Per capita units
Australia	Aus. dollar	1985	134,250	8,639
Hong Kong	HK dollar	1984	158,376	29,526
Indonesia	Rupiah (bns)	1983	49,231	317,005
Japan	Yen (bns)	1985	184,973	1,541,210
South Korea	Won (bns)	1984	40,381	952,382
Malaysia	Ringgit	1985	39,382	2,508
New Zealand	NZ dollar	1984	23,129	7,161
Philippines	Peso	1985	491,460	9,018
Singapore	S dollar	1984	38,733	15,316

Source: IMF, National statistics

TABLE 10.15 GOVERNMENT SPENDING

	Currency (millions)	Year	Total spending	% of GDP
Australia	Aus. dollar	1985	37,020	16.6
Hong Kong	HK dollar	1984	18,384	7.4
Indonesia	Rupiah (bns)	1983	7,791	10.9
Japan	Yen (bns)	1985	31,005	9.8
South Korea	Won (bns)	1984	7,137	10.6
Malaysia	Ringgit	1985	11,750	15.1
New Zealand	NZ dollar	1984	6,533	15.9
Philippines	Peso	1985	42,830	6.9
Singapore	S dollar	1984	4,307	7.8

Source: IMF, National statistics
Note: *Estimate

TABLE 10.16 GOVERNMENT FINANCE: BUDGET DEFICIT AS A PROPORTION OF GDP

	Currency (millions)	1984	%	1985	%
Australia	Aus. dollar	−7,905	3.9	−6,636	3.0
Hong Kong	HK dollar	−600[2]	0.2	100	0.0
Indonesia	Rupiah	−296,800	5.8	−281,800	n/a
Japan	Yen (bns)	−12,680[1]	4.3	−11,680[1]	3.7
South Korea	Won	−841,300	1.3	−945,000	1.5
Malaysai	Ringgit	−7,075	8.9	−5,999	7.7
New Zealand	NZ dollar	−3,209[2]	9.2	n/a	n/a
Philippines	Peso	−9,828	1.8	−11,188	1.8
Singapore	S dollar	2,088	5.4	595	1.6

Source: IMF, National statistics
Notes: [1]Value of government bond issues   [2]1983

182

TABLE 10.17   MERCHANDISE EXPORTS 1981–1985

US $ million, fob

	1981	1982	1983	1984	1985	
Australia	21,216	20,796	19,510	22,838	23,144	(est)
Hong Kong	2,147	1,954	2,063	2,838	30,154	
Indonesia	23,348	19,747	18,689	20,754	18,583	
Japan	149,520	137,660	145,470	168,290	173,920	
South Korea	20,671	20,879	23,204	26,335	26,442	
Malaysia	11,675	11,966	13,683	16,407	15,265	
New Zealand	5,527	5,240	5,651	5,481	5,722	(est)
Philippines	5,722	5,021	5,005	5,391	4,629	
Singapore	19,662	19,435	20,429	22,662	21,500	

Source: IMF, National statistics

TABLE 10.18   MERCHANDISE IMPORTS 1981–1985

US $ million, fob

	1981	1982	1983	1984	1985	
Australia	23,549	23,407	19,470	23,653	26,284	(est)
Hong Kong	2,432	2,196	2,252	2,864	29,821	
Indonesia	16,542	17,854	17,726	15,254	12,583	
Japan	129,560	119,580	114,010	124,030	117,920	
South Korea	24,299	23,473	24,967	27,461	26,461	
Malaysia	11,780	12,719	13,251	13,426	11,593	
New Zealand	5,529	5,363	5,492	5,612	5,738	
Philippines	7,946	7,667	7,490	6,070	5,111	
Singapore	25,785	26,196	26,252	26,734	24,535	

Sources: IMF, National statistics

183

TABLE 10.19   TRADE BALANCE

	1981	1982	1983	1984	1985
Australia	−2,333	−2,611	39	−815	−4,432 (est)
Hong Kong	−501	−365	−243	487	321
Indonesia	6,806	1,893	963	5,500	5,876
Japan	19,960	18,080	31,460	44,260	56,000
South Korea	−3,628	−2,594	−1,763	−1,036	−19
Malaysia	−105	−753	432	2,981	3,277
New Zealand	−2	−123	160	−131	−16 (est)
Philippines	−2,224	−2,646	−2,485	−679	−482
Singapore	−6,123	−6,762	−5,823	−4,071	−3,035

Source: IMF, National statistics

TABLE 10.20   CURRENT ACCOUNT BALANCE OF PAYMENTS, 1981–1985

US $ million						
	1980	1981	1982	1983	1984	1985
Australia	−4,148	−8,359	−8,290	−5,857	−8,304	−10,165
Hong Kong	−1,226	−1,599	−1,012	−500	1,410	2,179
Indonesia	2,864	−566	−5,324	−6,338	−2,114	−1,632
Japan	−10,750	4,770	6,850	20,800	35,000	49,260
South Korea	−5,321	−4,646	−2,650	−1,606	−1,372	−887
Malaysia	−285	−2,486	−3,601	−3,497	−1,660	−669
New Zealand	−807	−1,353	−1,476	−1,060	−1,425	−1,400 (est)
Philippines	−1,917	−2,096	−3,212	−2,751	−1,268	8
Singapore	−1,507	−1,478	−1,206	−819	−727	−253

Source: IMF, National statistics

TABLE 10.21   EXPORTS BY CATEGORY

Percentage of total exports

	Year	Agriculture	Mining & quarrying	Manufacturing
Australia	1982	23.9	26.2	49.9
Hong Kong	1983	0.6	0.2	99.2
Indonesia	1983	10.5	72.6	16.8
Japan	1983	0.4	0.2	99.4
South Korea	1981	5.2	0.4	94.4
Malaysia	1982	23.9	28.2	47.9
New Zealand	1983	15.8	0.8	83.4
Philippines	1982	12.0	10.6	77.3
Singapore	1983	8.0	1.8	90.3

Source: IMF, National statistics, Estimates

TABLE 10.22   IMPORTS BY CATEGORY

Percentage of total imports

	Year	Food, beverages, tobacco	Industrial supplies	Fuels	Mach-inery	Transport equipment	Consumer goods
Australia	1982	3.8	25.2	14.3	25.1	14.7	15.4
Hong Kong	1983	11.4	41.3	6.6	16.2	3.2	20.8
Indonesia	1983	7.1	30.6	24.8	26.6	8.4	2.2
Japan	1983	11.0	28.7	47.0	5.5	2.5	4.5
South Korea	1981	9.7	35.4	29.7	16.0	7.1	1.8
Malaysia	1982	9.7	28.4	15.0	29.4	10.3	6.4
New Zealand	1983	5.5	33.3	17.7	23.6	9.2	9.4
Philippines	1982	7.2	28.8	26.4	17.1	5.3	2.1
Singapore	1983	6.2	23.7	31.2	20.7	7.8	9.4

Source: IMF

TABLE 10.23 TOTAL EDUCATION EXPENDITURE AS % OF GNP AND TOTAL GOVERNMENT EXPENDITURE

	Year	US$ million	% Current	% Capital	% of GNP	% of government expenditure
Australia	1981	9,533.3	91.9	8.1	5.9	14.5
Hong Kong	1983	756.5	90.6	9.1	2.9	25.0
Indonesia	1981	1,434.7	—	—	2.2	9.3
Japan	1982	68,409.1	—	—	5.7	19.1
South Korea	1983	3,699.4	75.8	24.2	5.1	23.0
Malaysia	1982	1,959.5	78.8	21.2	7.5	22.0
New Zealand	1983	1,127.0	91.2	8.8	5.2	—
Philippines	1982	692.7	81.4	18.6	2.0	12.0
Singapore	1982	634.8	72.4	27.6	4.4	9.6

Source: United Nations, National statistics

TABLE 10.24 EXPORTS BY DESTINATION, 1985

US$ mn

	Industrialised countries	Africa	Other Asian	Europe	Middle East	USSR, East Europe	Others
Australia	57.9	1.0	22.3	1.2	7.7	3.4	1.1
Hong Kong	54.3	1.3	37.2	0.3	2.5	0.6	1.1
Indonesia	80.0	0.5	14.1	0.4	1.0	0.5	1.7
Japan	57.6	1.7	23.6	0.9	6.8	2.1	4.2
South Korea	70.0	2.1	13.3	1.4	6.2	0.0	3.3
Malaysia	54.6	0.3	38.3	0.7	1.8	1.4	0.4
New Zealand	66.2	1.7	15.0	1.5	6.1	2.5	2.4
Philippines	73.7	0.1	19.7	1.9	1.5	0.8	0.4
Singapore	46.5	2.3	39.4	1.1	5.6	1.3	2.0

Source: IMF, National statistics

TABLE 10.25   IMPORTS BY ORIGIN, 1985

US$ mn

	Industrial-ised countries	Africa	Other Asian	Europe	Middle East	USSR, East Europe	Others
Australia	77.9	0.7	11.6	0.5	4.2	0.2	1.3
Hong Kong	48.8	1.1	38.9	0.1	0.8	0.4	0.8
Indonesia	77.2	1.1	13.0	0.2	3.9	0.2	1.4
Japan	39.5	2.3	26.1	0.3	23.0	1.5	4.7
South Korea	64.5	1.0	12.0	1.2	9.5	0.0	5.5
Malaysia	61.5	0.4	29.9	0.2	3.9	0.4	0.9
New Zealand	81.1	0.6	11.4	0.3	3.1	0.2	1.3
Philippines	53.8	0.2	28.4	0.2	12.3	0.3	1.3
Singapore	49.0	0.8	31.9	0.3	13.9	0.2	0.5

Source: IMF, National sources

TABLE 10.26   FOREIGN INDEBTEDNESS AND LIQUIDITY, 1984/85

US$ mn

	Total foreign debt	% of GNP	% of foreign exchange receipts	International currency reserves
Australia	45,100	24.2	26.0	7,049
Hong Kong	6,180	19.0	0.2	—
Indonesia	23,500	29.4	15.7	4,702
Japan	74,300	55.8	—	22,283
South Korea	45,000	55.4	18.0	6,800
Malaysia	17,900	55.7	13.6	3,470
New Zealand	11,000	48.8	18.4	1,780
Philippines	25,400	77.6	37.5	574
Singapore	1,100	69.1	1.3	10,291

Source: National statistics

187

TABLE 10.27   HEALTH CARE FACILITIES

	Year	Hospital beds ('000)	Population per hospital bed	Population per doctor	Average daily calorie supply as % of require- ments (1983)
Australia	1984	166.0	94	444	140
Hong Kong	1985	24.6	4,593	1,210	128
Indonesia	1983/84	103.5	1,430	11,530	110
Japan	1982	1,400.0	94	780	124
South Korea	1981	63.8	636	2,990	126
Malaysia	1984	36.8	413	1,320	121
New Zealand	1984	31.6	102	635	130
Philippines	1984	70.6	753	7,970	116
Singapore	1985	8.0	316	1,150	121

Source: National statistics, World Bank, UNESCO

TABLE 10.28   TRANSPORT STATISTICS

	Main ports	International airports	Railways (km)	Total roads (km)	Paved (km)
Australia	15	4	39,065	865,000	450,000
Hong Kong	1	1	70	1,323	1,323
Indonesia	6	3	8,600	155,000	39,000
Japan	7	5	27,100	1,200,000	950,000
South Korea	4	1	6,007	50,850	16,350
Malaysia	9	5	20,917	43,818	33,980
New Zealand	4	3	4,273	96,000	45,000
Philippines	4	1	1,143	162,924	98,000
Singapore	1	1	26	2,569	2,569

Source: National statistics, Estimates

TABLE 10.29 MEDIA INDICATORS 1984

	Radios ('000)	per 1,000 population	TVs ('000)	per 1,000 population	Telephones ('000)	per 1,000 population
Australia	20,000	1,301	6,500	423	9,100	561.7
Hong Kong	2,710	510	1,195	225	2,350	438.1
Indonesia	22,000	138	3,500	22	9,114	5.7
Japan	85,000	713	66,342	556	62,000	512.4
South Korea	18,000	451	7,000	175	4,800	130.0
Malaysia	6,500	437	1,425	96	1,350	88.9
New Zealand	2,850	890	922	288	2,020	616.0
Philippines	2,342	45	1,350	26	850	15.6
Singapore	681	272	472	188	1,000	363.6

Source: UNESCO, National statistics

TABLE 10.30 TOURIST ARRIVALS

	1982 '000	1983 '000	1984 '000	1985 '000	Year	Visitors' expenditure (US$ million)
Australia	910	930	992	—	1984	752
Hong Kong	2,600	2,900	3,200	3,440	1985	1,900
Indonesia	592	639	683	—	1984	519
Japan	1,800	1,910	2,050	2,260	1985	2,100
South Korea	1,150	1,195	1,297	—	1984	366
Malaysia	2,400	2,681	2,950	—	1983	1,200
New Zealand	357	373	403	689	1985	600
Philippines	891	861	700	715	—	—
Singapore	2,900	2,800	2,991	2,910	1984	1,183

Source: National statistics, Estimates

LIST OF TABLES

193

INDEX

(Figures and Tables in **Bold**)

197